Panteras For The Road
By Henry Rasmussen

Published by Motorbooks International
Publishers and Wholesalers Incorporated,
Osceola, Wisconsin, U.S.A.
Copyright 1982 by Henry Rasmussen
Library of Congress number 82-8248.
ISBN 0 87938 157 4.
Printed in Hong Kong by South China
Printing Company
All rights reserved.

The Vallelunga was something new for De Tomaso; it was his first try at a Grand Touring car. The frame was of the spine type, just like his racing cars. The 1500 cc Cortina engine was actually a part of the frame. The four-cylinder power unit, from Ford's British subsidiary, produced 100 hp, although a 130 hp version was also available, according to the sales brochure. The Vallelunga, when first shown at the 1963 Turin Salon, was a Spyder, an open car. It weighed only 1,056 pounds. The more potent version was another fifty pounds lighter, and had a five-speed gearbox as opposed to the four-speed of the standard version. The body was designed by Fissore and also built by him in aluminum. When the Vallelunga finally became available in production form (it took until 1965), it had a coupe body. The prototype, still the work of Fissore, had the entire rear section removable for engine access. When Ghia took over the manufacture of the bodies, now made of fiberglass, the large plexiglass rear window provided this access. Price for the Spyder, when first shown, was advertised at $4,315 in Modena. This exciting-looking little GT car had all-independent suspension, four-wheel disc brakes and thirteen-inch Campagnolo magnesium wheels, six inches wide up front, seven inches in the back. The Vallelunga was really a racing car with a street body, and it was quite a performer for its engine size — zero-to-sixty came in less than nine seconds. Anywhere between fifty and 180 are thought to have been made — a truly limited production automobile.

Affectionately known as the "Goose," the Mangusta had superb Italian styling combined with American go! Giugiaro, then with Ghia, designed the taut, tight body on a 98.4-inch wheelbase. The 43.4-inch low beauty was first seen at the 1966 Turin Salon. The prototype shown there was of fiberglass and had an aluminum engine, a De Tomaso-produced Ford V-8 replica, reportedly with an output of around 500 hp. The production version, available from 1967, had a steel/aluminum body built by Ghia and a standard cast-iron Ford Windsor engine. It was mounted midships, pointed fore and aft, displaced 302 cid, produced 230 hp, and had a cut-out at 5200 rpm. The Ford engine was a practical solution to cost and torque; there was no fuss at low speed, no expensive maintenance, and no excuses up to the top speed of 120-150 mph. The acceleration time of just over six seconds from zero to sixty needed no alibi either. Luggage went both up front, as well as in a deep compartment ahead of the left rear wheel. The fifteen-inch Campagnolo wheels were seven inches wide up front; eight in the rear. Tires were by Dunlop and measured 185 and 235. Weight was around 3,000 pounds. The Mangusta was sold in the United States by British Motor Car Distributors in San Francisco. The price was $11,685, including air conditioning, five-speed ZF transmission, limited-slip rear end, electric windows, four-wheel power-assisted disc brakes — but no front bumpers. The car was meant to be driven — not to be parked! Exactly 401 cars were made between 1967 and 1971.

Vallelunga

Mangusta

Although inspiration for the Pantera came from the Mangusta, it was an all-new car, styled by Tom Tjaarda and engineered by Gianpaolo Dallara. The new 351 cid Cleveland V-8 Ford provided 310 hp (European version, 330 hp). Maximum rpm was 5400. The slippery body had the low drag-coefficient of 0.29 and was a real eye-catcher. With the available power, the aerodynamic body gave the Pantera a zero-to-sixty time of around seven seconds (just over six for the European version) and a top speed of 150 plus. The new Campagnolo wheels were fifteen inches in diameter, seven inches wide in the front and eight in the back. Tires were by Michelin, 185 and 215. Wheelbase was the same as the Mangusta, but the height of the United States version Pantera had grown two inches. Weight was around 3,200 pounds, up a little. Again, the five-speed ZF transmission was used. The all-steel monocoque was built by Vignale but carried Ghia's emblem on the fenders. The easiest way to recognize the first seventy-five cars is by their round doorknobs; later cars had square ones. All had the small chrome bumpers, until the L-model came. There was a small space for luggage up front, but most of it went in the back, behind the engine. Price was just under $10,000 at introduction in 1971. Magazine road tests were not wholly favorable; the eye-appeal was unanimously acknowledged; the power was equally cheered; but the living area was very tight for American drivers. There were also things like overheating and undercooling — in short, it lacked development. Still, it was a lot of car for the money.

From 1973, the Pantera was not quite the same. It was now called the "L" model. "L" stands for Lusso, which means luxury in Italian. It also came to stand for Legislation. Tough new government regulations — smog, bumpers and more — had arrived. It meant that new bumpers had to be designed for the Pantera. Up front, they blended very well with the styling; even added to the sleekness. The general specifications stayed the same; it still had the 351 Cleveland, the five-speed ZF transmission, the monocoque construction, the wheelbase, the four-wheel disc brakes, the wheel size, and so on. But the tires changed — and not for the better — although that was what Ford had in mind when it asked Goodyear to develop a tire especially for the Pantera. It was called Arriva. C60X15 was used up front; H60X15 in the rear. There was, unfortunately, also another change in power; compression was lowered from 8.6:1 to 8.0:1; power dropped to 248 hp. And, of course, performance also dropped; zero-to-sixty took almost seven seconds now and top speed was 140 mph plus. The bumpers added length, but also weight; seventy-five pounds for a total of 3,280 pounds. In spite of the Lincoln/Mercury dealers, who really didn't know how to handle a sports car, the Pantera sold relatively well. The price was now $11,500. But, the Pantera had run its course; Ford wanted out. Between 6,000 and 7,000 cars had been built between 1971 and 1974, depending on whose figures you read.

Pantera

Pantera L

This is the European GT5, a street car. It takes its name from the FIA Group 5 racing category which requires silhouette consistency in the body relative to stock, but allows flares to accommodate the larger tires as well as certain aerodynamic aides. The Pantera raced with the FIA Group 5 cars, but did not do well. Need we repeat that it takes money to research and develop a racing car based on a production automobile? It doesn't just happen! The car featured here is a 1981 model. The basic statistics are the same as the old Pantera of the early seventies. Now, the cars are built by De Tomaso Automobili, located on Via Emilia Ovest 1250, in Modena. The protuberances, however, make the car look very different; low and wide front air dam, with built-in fog lights; very wide fender flares with an air intake in front of the rear wheel; skirts to connect the fenders; two vents on the hood for improved airflow out of the hood, and a fresh air side scoop that replaces the previous faked louvers behind the side window completes the picture. The wheels are the Campagnolo ones developed for De Tomaso's racing effort. They are ten inches wide up front and thirteen in the rear. Pirelli P7's are fitted, 285/40 and 345/35. Performance-wise, the engine delivers 330 hp, which translates to a top speed of 168 mph and a zero-to-sixty time of just over six seconds. The particular car featured here has a v-shaped rear wing. Firms like Porsche have promoted their Group 5 cars to the hilt. Pantera, without the victories, cannot do that successfuly.

The Pantera featured here is a 1982 European version GT5. Since the specifications are identical to the car featured on the left, except that the car above has a roof spoiler rather than a wing, this column will deal with the Pantera as it is presently imported to the United States. Three models are marketed in America, and they are visually identical to the three versions offered by De Tomaso in Europe: The GTS, the GT4 and the GT5. In order to meet United States specifications, Panteramerica, the United States importer, has established all modifications required to comply with regulations, and has worked these out with De Tomaso so that everything is done at the factory before the cars are shipped. Performance is down a bit, from 330 hp to 300 hp. Top speed is down to 156 mph. The zero-to-sixty time is seven seconds. The Pantera of today is a much improved car, with handcrafted body work, with handcrafted leather interior and with the bugs taken out. United States prices start at $46,600 for the GTS and rise to $54,995 for the GT5. *Popular Mechanics* did a "Million Dollar" test comparing the Pantera GTS, BMW, M1, Porsche 928, Lamborghini Countach, Ferrari 512 Boxer, Ferrari 308 GTSi and several others. If you go back to the makes listed above, that is how they finished in a combination of tests at the Ontario Motor Speedway. The magazine, in its resume of the results, concluded that since the Pantera had finished second or third in every category and since it cost only half of the price of the second place car, this was reason enough to place it on top overall. Not bad for the new old Pantera.

Pantera GT5 Custom

Pantera GT5

This car was built by Hall Pantera of Bellflower, California. It is not a Super Pantera. It has riveted-on fiberglass flares — original factory equipment — not the metal flares that are put on the Super Pantera. Under the flares are ten-inch wheels front and thirteen-inch wheels rear. Pirelli P-7 tires are mounted — 285/40 front and 345/35 rear. The paint job on this car is the result of the same painstaking process as used on the Super Pantera. The car is dismantled, part by part. The metal is dipped and stripped of paint. The chassis is reinforced and re-welded. The body is metal-finished. This is not a lead-shed! Metal finishing is handwork done by artisans. To take a given piece of metal and be able to stretch or shrink the size of it requires a true craftsman. The car is primed and left to cure for ten days. Then comes the block sanding. The paint is usually a stock factory color; but an enamel paint is used. It is harder to work with. The first coats of paint go on and are left to sit in the sun for six weeks. Then, it is color sanded with 600-grit paper. More paint and another six weeks in the sun for curing. Then 1000-grit sanding. The finish is now show quality. The mechanics of this car have not been touched, so it is a stock Pantera; which is not all that shabby! Seven seconds, zero-to-sixty, will keep you ahead of most of the crowd. And a top speed of 150 mph is more than adequate for that quick jaunt to the country estate. The louvers front and rear are not just for looks — they aid the cooling.

"The hot one is hotter." Chevrolet once advertised their cars this way. Ironically, some Pantera owners have put the big-block Chevrolet engine (454 cid) in the Pantera. Even more ironic, they don't go any faster than the Ford 351 cid. Now, take this Super Pantera; its 351 cid engine is blueprinted to a fine hone. Output is 475 hp. The maximum rev limited is 7,000 rpm, due to a special camshaft. Performance? How about a top speed of 180 mph and zero-to-sixty around four seconds? The exhaust headers look like the Cam-Am Challenge type, big spaghetti tubes stretched out to achieve the equal length necessary for top performance. Extra cooling is obtained through the multiple cooling louvers in the hood and trunk. Don't forget that the radiator is mounted up front. It needs to have vents for the air to escape. Those flares are wide and they cover big wheels — ten inches up front and thirteen rear. Tires are 285/40 Pirelli P-7 front and 345/35 rear. The rest of the car is just like the normal Super Pantera offered by Hall Pantera. The weight of the car is no more than the standard Pantera, 3,200 pounds. The large flares and the wide, low tires give it that really mean look; seems like it is ready to jump at you. The flat black paint on the hood and trunk is like the GTS Pantera. The black paint on the lower section of the car is a trick that stylists use to lower the car visually. This was also used on the GTS. Even with flares and trick paint, the original good looks of the Tjaarda-designed Pantera comes through — sleek and purposeful.

Pantera Showcar

Hall Pantera GTS

Gary Hall of Bellflower, California, produces a better Pantera — the Super Pantera. He takes a good, used Pantera and rebuilds it, doing it the way it should have been done in the first place. The engine is blueprinted, still the 351 cid version, but it now puts out 400 hp. Big-bore/equal-length headers are used. Hall finishes the car with braided stainless steel lines on all water and air-conditioning lines. The inner fender panels are stainless steel, which doesn't rust. The paint is stripped completely. Any sloppiness in the body work is metal finished. Hood, trunk and doors are aligned. Paint is thirty coats of enamel, put on slowly, over a period of about twelve weeks. Koni shock absorbers are installed, as are Pirelli P-7 tires. An important change is made in the hood. There are two vents cut in. The early Panteras didn't have this modification. The Pantera has the radiator up front. Air came in under the front bumper. But it had no place to exit. The latest factory Panteras now also have this feature, but Hall's Pantera was first. Now there is no overheating at idle or slow speeds. An added precaution is a special high-flow radiator. Eight-inch wheels front and ten-inch rear are mounted with 225/50 tires front and 275/55 rear. Resulting zero-to-sixty times are six seconds; top speed is 160 mph. A prospective buyer can choose between the Group 3, 4 or 5 look. Group 3 is stock; Group 4 has mild fender flares and Group 5 has flares, skirts and air dam. There's even a wing available. These cars will look like the ones cataloged by the factory. The interior is luxurious, upholstered in leather. Prices start at about $66,000.

The turbocharged engine is not new. A patent for the turbo goes back to 1905. Aircraft used turbos in World War II. The Indianapolis cars tried turbos in the fifties. The Oldsmobile F-85 and Chevrolet Corvair had turbos in the early sixties. Porsche came on strong in 1972 with the turbo and in 1973 with the twin turbo 917/30. The turbo uses exhaust gasses recirculated back to the engine. The early drawback was turbo lag — that awful second or two before the turbo took off. A simple waste-gate solved that problem. The Twin-Turbo Pantera featured here is a one-off car. It is pretty standard in specifications, except, with the turbo installed, the horsepower jumps to 750. The zero-to-sixty time is almost quicker than you can measure. Since speed is determined by rear end ratio and cams, top speed is only 160 mph. It will do 130 mph in the quarter-mile, yet is smooth on the street. Two AiResearch Turbo units are used. Utilizing a standard pump fuel, the turbos produce about a six-pound boost each. The wheels are eight-inches up front and ten-inches in the rear. Tires are Firestone Rain racing tires. Just for the record, the basic engine is still the good old 351 cid Cleveland, originally engineered by Bill Gay. The Cleveland engine was made for the Mustang-Cougar and Torino-Montego. It had enlarged ports, larger valves, closer tolerances, higher rpm capacity and a 750-cubic-foot-per-minute four-barrel carburetor. It was a solid engine. This red beauty looks perfectly stock, except the black chrome, and really is stock, until you lift the rear deck and take out the removable luggage compartment.

Hall Super Pantera

Pantera Twin Turbo

"My wife told me to take the GTS out and race it," said Gary Hall of Hall Pantera. "It was the third Super Pantera I built. I sold it once and traded it back again later. I rebuilt the car completely." The event was a time trial at the old Ontario Motor Speedway. Hall turned in the fastest time at the meet. The car still has the stock suspension, and the dimensions are identical to a regular Pantera. The engine is basically the 351 cid Ford V-8. Power is up to about 650 hp and the fuel is methanol. The zero-to-sixty time is irrelevant, but the quarter-mile speed is 139 mph in about ten seconds. Top speed is estimated at 225 mph. Hall has installed a chin spoiler and a rear lip spoiler to prevent takeoff. The tire and wheel combination was a trial and error effort. Hall uses Goodyear racing tires. The front tires are eleven inches wide, twenty-three inches tall, on sixteen inch rims. The rear tires are twenty-seven inches tall, fifteen-and-a-half wide, and mounted on nineteen inch rims. Outside of the spoilers, the wheel flares are the only body modifications. The tuned exhaust system uses large spaghetti tubes of equal length. The weight of the race car is about 2,750 pounds. The reduction in weight is due to aluminum doors, hood and trunk as well as a lightweight Lexan windshield. At Riverside Raceway, Hall runs the race car in time trials on the regular racetrack at times that are competitive to recent IMSA GTU class times. Hall says, "If someone had put some dollars into the car when it was new, it could have been competitive. The 351 engine was one of the finest racing engines."

If you can't have your name on a car as builder, the next best thing is to set a speed record. That was what Mike Cook, of Carson, California did. He knew the Pantera's slippery styling would be perfect; the drag-coefficient is 0.29. The Southern California Timing Association rules for the GT class dictate that a stock body configuration be used. Modifications were made only in the fact that a roll bar and a fire protection system were installed. The engine and the tires are the areas where the obvious changes were made. The engine is still the 351 cid Ford V-8. A Boss crankshaft is used with Carello steel rods, as well as 13:1 forged pistons, roller cam, titanium valves and rocker arms and high port heads. Horsepower is about 650; rev limit is in the range of 8,500-9,000 rpm. Fuel injection is used. All of these changes are allowed in the rule book. The tires present a problem. It seems that Firestone made the Bonneville-type tires quite a while ago. There is no new supply of tires; therefore, old tires must be used. By old, try over forty years old! The tires are hard as rock and cracked; but if you want to go fast, there is no alternative. The front tires are twenty-three-inches tall and very narrow. Since the engine is midship, and the car is under constant acceleration, weight on the front is low and there is no need for a large patch of rubber on the ground. The rear tires are thirty-one-inches tall and also narrow, as far as rear tires go these days. How does it move? Does 185 mph in the standing mile sound impressive? You better believe it! That was at El Mirage Dry Lake, California. At Bonneville, Utah, it did 195 mph.

Pantera Racing Car

Pantera Record Car

The Best of Both Worlds

Curiously, when the first advertisements for the new Pantera appeared, the text, studded with superlatives, did not mention the origin of the engine. The Italian bodywork was hailed as "craftsmanship at its highest level." The gearbox was praised as "built to racing specifications in Germany." Nothing was said about the engine being American.

In later ads however, the theme "the best of both worlds" was introduced — referring to the merits of combining Italian styling by Ghia ("an aerodynamically sculptured body") with American power by Ford ("one of the most highly regarded engines in its class").

No one, not even the most discerning among connoisseurs, could deny that the sleek styling of the Pantera, so exquisitely protrayed in the ads, was on the level with the best in the field. Based on the most advanced ideas of the new Italian school, as expressed by Giugiaro in the Mangusta, it was now developed and given a new personality by Tjaarda. The Pantera was one of the best styling achievements in the mid-engine category. There was no question about that fact.

But the engine did pose a problem. Obviously, this was the reason its origin went unmentioned in the early ads. But, it was only a problem of image. Practically, it was more reliable, more serviceable and, as many present day owners are discovering, more easily tuned than the purebred engines of a Ferrari, a Maserati or a Lamborghini. Ford engines had been tested on the grueling proving grounds of American stock car racing, as well as in the most taxing European endurance events, and found to be competitive. Granted, the Ford engines were never as intriguingly complex as its purebred counterparts — for good and for bad — they had certainly proved to be winners.

Personal preferences aside, the Pantera belongs right up there alongside the most excitingly beautiful of sports cars — thanks to its Italian heritage. And yes, right up there alongside the fastest and most powerful ever developed for the road — thanks to its American heritage.

One can forever argue the importance of purity of origin, but it is impossible to argue with the sound and the feeling of that roar of brute power exploding behind you when you let a Pantera loose...

Obviously forming the letter T – for De Tomaso – the hieroglyphical design on the badge is said to be based on the letter I – for Alessandro's wife Isabella. The blue and white comes from the flag of his native Argentina. The badge was first seen on De Tomaso's racing cars of the late fifties. Above, the badge adorns the grille of a Mangusta and, to the right, that of a Pantera. On the opposite page, it decorates the hub of a Pantera wheel. Notice the small symbol stamped into each lug nut – a feature found only on the very early cars. Below, the second-generation Pantera script, here seen on a pinstriped show car.

Born and educated in Detroit, but working in Italy, Pantera stylist Tom Tjaarda succeeded in creating an exotic sports car in the true Italian tradition. Previously, during his four years with Pininfarina, he had worked on, among other projects, the Ferrari 365 California. The Pantera was conceived at Ghia, where Tjaarda had taken over as head of styling in 1968. To the left, the most characteristic detail of the Pantera shape – the rear deck. The overall design was exceptionally pleasing and harmonious; emphasizing, rather than ignoring, the mid-engined location. Above, on early cars, silver pinstriping highlighted the fake louvers behind the small side window. On later cars, the gas filler cap was concealed here. Another feature, also unique to the earliest cars, was the round doorknob, pictured to the right. The photograph to the upper right shows the aerodynamic drop-shape of the mirror used on European version Panteras.

An Ordinary Visit to the Factory

Part One

If you are a Pantera enthusiast, and a visit to the factory in Italy is high on your list of priorities, you may want to think twice before you take the trip. Or, at least, you should know what to expect...

Now, remembering my own experience when visiting the De Tomaso factory last spring, I can't quite recall what grand things I had thought would happen once I got there. Maybe, since I was working on a book about the Pantera, and my arrival had been announced in advance, the idea that I would receive some kind of red carpet treatment might have planted itself in my mind.

Although, I must admit, after what happened in Milano, it is just as likely that a negative attitude had taken a hold of me even before I arrived at the factory.

My Swedish friend Tomas Wenner, who lives in Switzerland, accompanied me on this trip. We had driven down from Zurich in his beautiful BMW 3.0 CSi. After staying overnight in a motel along the Autostrada, we arrived in Milano at the end of the lunch hour traffic rush. A series of well-timed dashes between ricocheting Fiats brought us to an eating establishment Tomas knew from before.

We were the last to be seated. This meant the staff could give us plenty of attention; three waiters instead of one were assigned to us. Normally that would have made for a pleasant reversal of roles, but this time it only meant the beginning of our troubles.

Tomas, who had picked up his Italian on the streets of Milano, just as he had gotten the hang of his French on the beaches of St. Tropez, soon had the waiters involved in a conversation on the subject of

The ultimate road machine? Maybe not, but quite a handful, and quite adequate even for Italian Autostradas. Even though the sign covering the license plate reads GT4, the car is actually a GT5. The sign was not placed there to identify the car, but to hide the identity of the owner. Although, it is hard to see how anyone can remain anonymous in this car. Admittedly, if he travels fast enough, no one will be able to catch a glimpse of the driver. The basic car, as mentioned, is a GT5 – the latest development of the Pantera by the De Tomaso factory. This particular car has been modified with, among other things, a handsome rear wing, designed and manufactured by the factory. (Photographs by the author.)

soccer. Many Swedish players had become successful professionals in Italy. We found that some of them were remembered as heroes, and Tomas, amazingly, knew many stories about their early careers in Sweden; stories he now told with great virtuosity.

The excitement of the conversation spread like a contagious disease. The group of white-jacketed, black-cravated waiters surrounding our table grew steadily, which brought the benefit of unasked-for trays of cheese and ham as well as a bottle of Barolo.

It would all have stayed amusing if I hadn't opened by big mouth and changed the subject to boxing. Now, in addition to the loud chatter of Italian, accompanied by all the hand gestures, we also had a variety of uppercuts, left jabs and right hooks flying in the air as Primo Carnera's or Joe Louis' or Rocky Marciano's favorite punches were demonstrated.

As if that wasn't enough, I opened my big mouth even wider to mention the name of Ingemar Johanson, the Swedish World Champion, telling how he, right here in Milano, had fought an Italian and knocked him out through the ropes in the second round. No? Is that possible? Who was that? Naturally, at that crucial point, I couldn't recall the name of this unfortunate fighter. So it came out sounding like a lie. No one had ever heard of this fight. Knocked him out through the ropes? No! That couldn't be true! It was a downright impolite thing to say! The conversation ended in silence.

Unexpectedly, one of the waiters afterwards returned to our table to tell us about a major boxing event scheduled for that same evening. The arena was located in the outskirts of Milano and he drew a map with instructions how to get there and also recommended a hotel. I have never been able to ascertain if he meant to do us a favor or if he actually placed a retaliatory curse on us.

When, later that afternoon, we decided to attend this boxing extravaganza, it somehow took us more than two hours to get there; the map sent us detouring forever. When we finally found the place, it turned out to be a very minor event, held in a small gym that could seat no more than a couple hundred spectators. The hotel seemed at first to be all right, with many of the fighters also staying there.

But, somehow, the same fighters we had met at the hotel before the event, the same fighters we had gotten to know, the same fighters we had discussed strategy with, those same fighters all turned out to be

(continued on overleaf)

Photographed just outside Modena and only a few miles from the De Tomaso factory, this potent looking creation rests in classic surroundings – the narrow, poplar-lined country road could have looked the same decades ago when racing's pioneers tested their primitive machinery in this neighborhood. Today it is the setting for the ultimate from De Tomaso – the Pantera GT5. The example featured here was the only completed car available at the time of our visit and it was reluctantly released for photography, provided owner and specifications were kept confidential. Thus it is not known what hides beneath the sleek silver skin – but what can be seen on the outside is certainly exciting enough. The flares, skirts and air dam are fiberglass and patterned after Group 5 racing cars. The wing is the creation of De Tomaso's own engineers. Test driver Ivano Cornia told us it improved traction and stability but that it also lowered top speed somewhat.

losers. Not only was it disenchanting to watch them take a beating, but, afterwards in the hotel, it was downright depressing, watching them file through the revolving door, their faces swollen and cut, their eyes nailed to the floor, their trainers carrying the gear with a humility unusual for that breed, their managers chewing on burnt-out cigars; and then worst of all, watching those losers line up outside the phone booth in the lobby, waiting quietly for their turn to call their mothers and girlfriends with the bad news. If you have never stayed in a hotel full of losers, you don't know what I'm talking about. It is very bad for your attitude.

The morning after — an overcast Sunday — we took off for Modena, traveling on the main Autostrada connecting Milano with Bologna. We found the wide open, monotonously flat Po Valley an uninviting place this time of the year; the vineyards were still dead, the fields still lay unplanted and gray and a bitter cold wind blew constantly.

As we neared Modena, we noticed a blue-gray silhouette of low hills to the south. According to my bearings, that would be on the far side of the city, just beyond Maranello and the Ferrari factory.

We found the De Tomaso plant easy to get to, located just off the Autostrada. The facility seemed to be the last vestige of an industrial sector on the outskirts of the city. An old, two-lane thoroughfare passed alongside the property and continued on to the east, cutting through open fields lined with naked poplars and old farm houses.

Since it was Sunday, we decided to just stop on the street in front of the complex, which consisted of three main buildings, all constructed of gray concrete. The first, apparently housing showroom and offices, was a modern one-story creation with large windows. A huge De Tomaso sign protruded from the roof. Behind this building was another, twice as tall, with that typical jagged sawblade-type roof line — apparently the main assembly hall. Behind these two buildings was a third, lower and older, apparently a warehouse. It all seemed smaller than expected and was rather unkept looking, with lawns that had gone into weed, with butchered and rusting vehicles that had been left to die between the buildings. The entire place was rather disappointing — gray, deserted, windswept — especially on a day like this.

For the night, we registered at Hotel Europa, in Maranello, arriving there at dusk. From our window, we could look out over the fortress-like compound of the Ferrari factory. It too lay deserted.

The fiberglass flares and skirts, pictured to the left, are standard GT5 features. On this custom car, the front of the flares have been rounded off, creating a smooth transition into the spoiler, as can be seen in the large photograph at the right. Other individual changes include the darker shade of paint applied to the body below the crease in the side panel, as well as a hood mounted rack of five driving lights. These lights are stowed in the luggage compartment, and are only mounted when needed for fast driving in the dark. The mounting holes are noticeable beside the headlight buckets in the picture above. (Photographs by the author.)

An Ordinary Visit to the Factory

Part Two

The next morning arrived with more of the same icy wind and more of the same gray sky; nature still denied us any signs of the approaching spring. Over at the De Tomaso factory, things were only a fraction more exciting than they had been the previous day.

Inside the front door, we found ourselves standing in a small room that served both as an entrance and as a reception area. If I recall correctly, there was a desk in there, but no one was sitting by it, and no one acknowledged our presence. Straight ahead, behind glass partitions, was a large room with several desks and filing cabinets as well as a few clerks. To the left, also through glass partitions, we could see what looked like an engineering studio. There were several large drafting tables in the room, and a couple of Moto-Guzzi or Benelli motorcycles, but no one was working in there. To the right was a small waiting room, or conference room, with a low table and three or four lounge chairs. Through the open door we could see that his room too was empty.

While we waited for someone to notice us, the only object for our eyes to focus on was a small photograph on one of the walls in the reception area. It captured, for posterity, the occasion in the early seventies when the 2500th Pantera rolled off the production line.

After a long wait, we noticed that a woman on the other side of the glass partitions straight ahead, was indeed aware of our presence. She took her time to finish whatever she was doing, then came out, reluctantly, asking in good English what we wanted. She was sweet and mild-mannered, but let us know in so many unspoken words that visitors were not especially welcome. After all, we have a job to do here, she

The photograph to the left commemorates the occasion of the 2500th Pantera completed. The picture has been cropped; there are more workers gathered around the car, all saluting the man in the dark suit, their boss, Alessandro De Tomaso. To the left of him stands Aurelio Bertocchi, the general manager. Pictured on top of this page, are some of De Tomaso's offspring, stored in the main assembly hall. The photographs above and right show the GT5, but are mainly reproduced here to help give the viewer an idea, although incomplete and unflattering, of De Tomaso's facilities in Modena. (Photographs courtesy of De Tomaso Automobili and Winston S. Goodfellow.)

seemed to say, without actually saying it. We explained to her who we were and what we wanted and that the visit had been set up the previous week during a phone conversation with Mister Bertocchi, the general manager. She told us to wait right here, and all we could do was to follow her with our eyes, looking through the glass partitions as she zig-zagged her way between desks and filing cabinets to finally disappear through a distant door.

We returned to the photograph on the wall. About a dozen mechanics had been lined up, surrounding a Pantera — a GTS. The car was about to be rolled down from a portion of the assembly line scaffolding. The mechanics all held drinking glasses in their hands, filled with champagne — presumably — ready to propose a toast to the continued success of the Pantera project — presumably.

The sweet and mild-mannered woman finally returned. She explained that Ingegnere Bertocchi was very, very busy, and that he under no circumstances could see us. She did not offer a solution to this dilema. Instead she looked like she expected us to go away. Her attitude did not seem to sit well with Tomas, who, switching to his most impressive Italian, proceeded to explain to her in detail who Mister Rasumssen was and how far he had traveled to come here. She did not seem the slightest bit impressed, which did not surprise me, but she did at least suggest that we come back in the afternoon. Although, she said there was absolutly no guarantee that he could see us at that time either. Ingegnere Bertocchi is a very, very busy man!

Suddenly, just at that point, I could feel the negative attitude that had been building up inside me explode into anger and come rushing through my veins like turbocharged exhaust gasses. Only the sight of this sweet little mild-mannered woman in front of me kept me from committing a violent crime.

I firmly, but calmly, repeated the objectives of our visit: an interview with Mister Bertocchi, a tour of the premises, permission to photograph the facilities and access to a brand new Pantera for photography off the factory grounds. I asked her to again confront Mister Bertocchi with these demands. I could imagine how the poor woman must feel. With Tomas' threatening six-foot-two frame hovering above her out here, and an overworked and possibly irritated boss awaiting her in the back, the expression on her face — a classic case of frustration — was understandable.

(continued on overleaf)

Rain and snow made for a tough photographic assignment and a rough virgin journey for this, the latest, car to roll out through the factory gates at De Tomaso. Swiss enthusiast Karl Albrecht owns this GT5, chassis number 9222. He placed the order in September 1981 and took delivery in March 1982 – the same day it was posed for these photographs. Karl made several trips to the factory during the assembly, making sure all the extras he had ordered were actually being put in. Having owned five Panteras before, he feels this will be his last. After all, how could he possibly get a better one.

When the woman finally returned, she had a short, round faced, energetic-looking gentleman behind her. Ingegnere Bertocchi, she said, introducing him formally, then stepping aside. Mister Bertocchi gave the immediate impression of being a very sympathetic man, but in order to benefit from this side of him, you apparently should never meet him at the factory, for here he seemed to be charged almost to the breaking point.

Mister Bertocchi asked again what we wanted, curiously, as if he didn't know already. We reminded him of the phone conversation, and repeated what we had hoped to accomplish here. During this explanation, his attention was divided between a stack of papers in his hand and two distinguished looking gentlemen who had emerged from his office in the back, now apparently waiting to continue an interrupted discussion. They looked like they represented oil-money, but I could have been mistaken.

If we came back in the afternoon, Mister Bertocchi said, he could give us a tour of the plant. But under no circumstances could we take any pictures in the assembly area. Absolutely not. The camera would have to stay here. I was extremely disappointed, which I told him. I explained that I had hoped to fill an entire section in my book with pictures from the factory. But Mister Bertocchi was firm. No pictures! Please understand! Absolutley not! What about an interview? Behind his bold-framed glasses, Mister Bertocchi's eyes darted observantly between us, the papers and the two gentlemen. Is an interview necessary? What do you want to know? We have brochures to give you. I decided to drop that subject for the moment and try another. Can you let us have a Pantera to photograph? We don't have any cars now. What? No cars? Not one? No, not at the present time. Sorry. He glanced over in the direction of the oil-money men again. Come back in the afternoon, and I'll show you around! He said this with a polite but firm smile and was suddenly on his way, in an instant beyond our reach, gone behind the glass partitions.

The sweet and mild-mannered woman bid us farewell as if she didn't expect to see us again. Tomas and I went out to his BMW, utterly disillustioned, started it up and turned it east on Via Emilia. As we passed the place we had thought would make such a nice location for the shooting, ironically enough, the sun broke through the hazy spring sky, spreading a warm cast across the fields and farmhouses. But we had already decided to forget about the whole thing.

If the present-day offering of new Panteras seems a bit confusing, it is only because any combination goes – it is up to the customer. Today's car is without question much improved. Cosmetically, one only has to take a look at the sumptous leather interior, pictured to the left. The awesome-looking GT5, to the lower right seen in both light and dark color schemes, seems to make up the bulk of today's production. Above right, a GT5, chassis number 9020, belonging to a Swiss enthusiast. This car has riveted-on spoiler, flares and skirts. It also has extra air-scoops just ahead of the rear wheels. (Photographs by Winston S. Goodfellow and Motorsport-Fotos.)

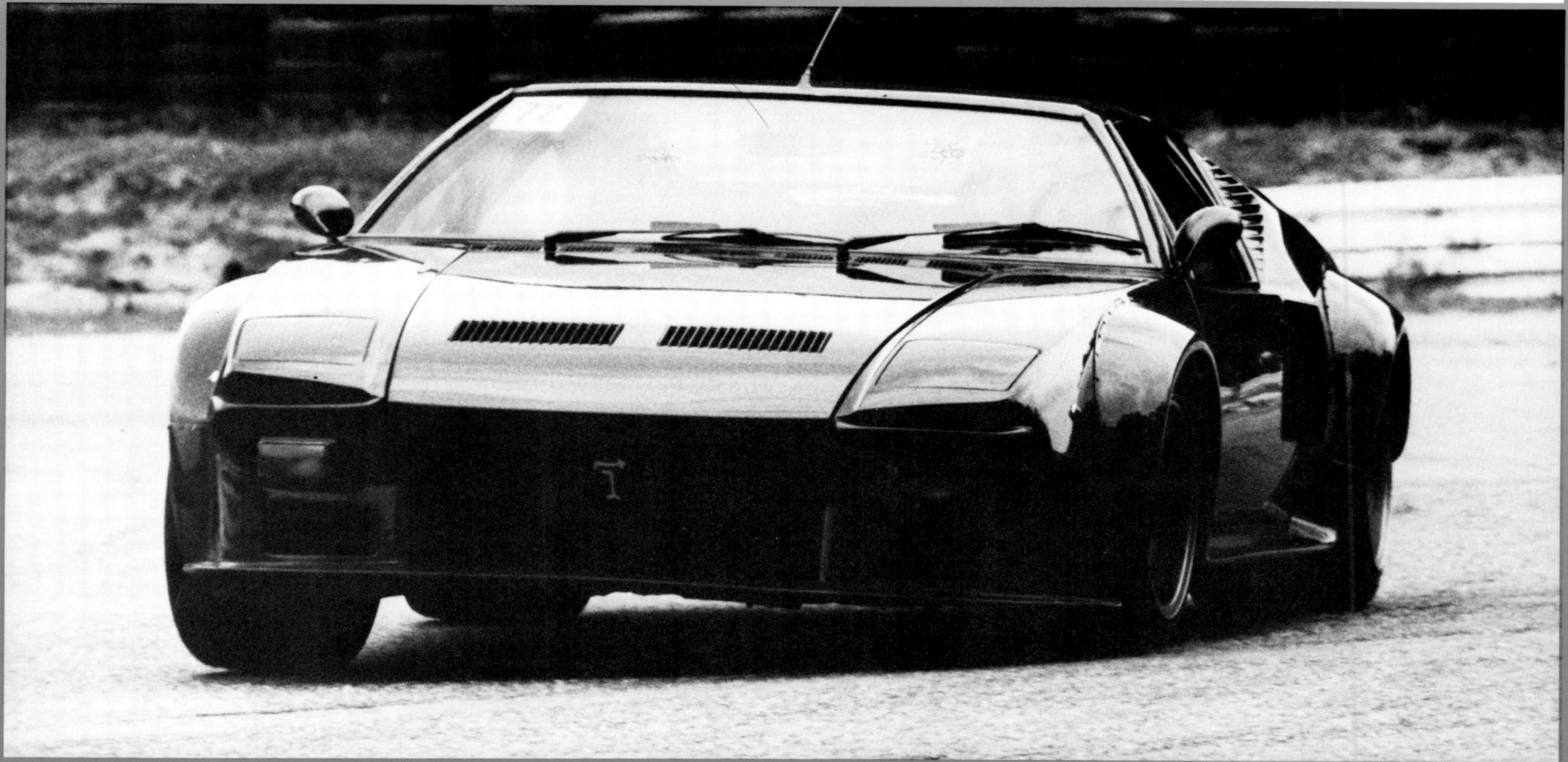

PANTERA
GT5
DETOMASO

PANTERA
GT5
DETOMASO

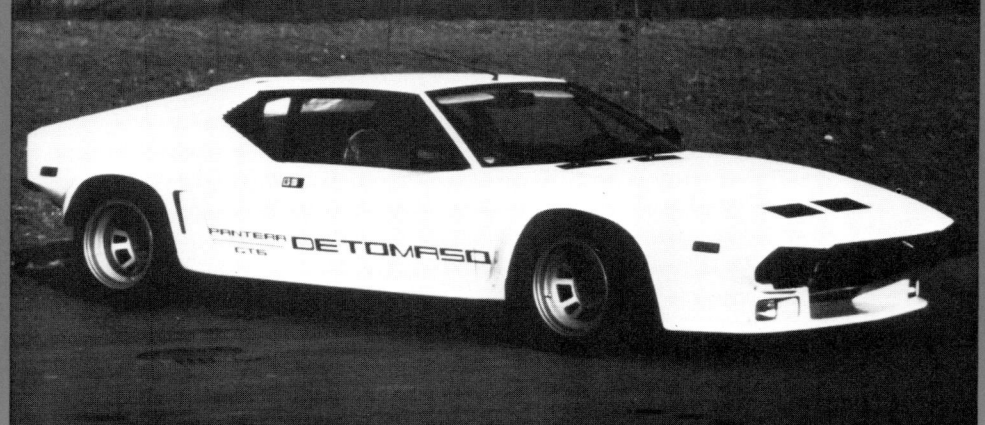

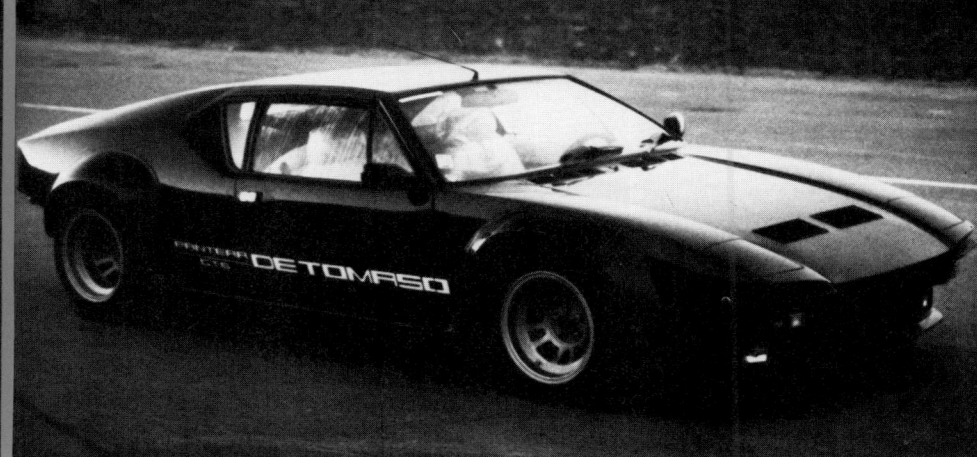

An Ordinary Visit to the Factory

Part Three

During the delicious lunch at Arnaldo's, our pessimistic outlook was moderated, and we thought it worthwhile to return to the factory after all.

Our sweet and mild-mannered friend seemed quite acceptable to us now when we knew what to expect, and we weren't at all surprised when she told us that Ingegnere Bertocchi was too busy to show us around and that she would have the honor instead.

Inside the assembly hall, I was at first overwhelmed by the apparent chaos of the scene; bits and pieces were scattered everywhere. It was like entering an antique shop: You were unable to focus on one particular object because of the complexity of the total picture. After that initial reaction, two things struck me as odd: The absence of cars and the absence of workers. Although there were some of both, the tranquility of the scene was in total contrast to what I had expected. It was as if we had arrived on the lunch-break or during the vacation shut-down.

First to emerge from this confusing picture was a line-up of cars immediately to our left. It turned out to be a collection of early De Tomaso creations.

First in the line-up were a couple of Formula racing cars, if I recall correctly. Then came a red Vallelunga. But not just any Vallelunga. This was one of the first few Fissore-built prototype coupes. Then followed two important, but never developed, sports racing car projects; first, the Ghia/De Tomaso 70P, then, the Competizione 2000 — both painted red. Then came the 1970 Formula One car, complete with rear wing, impressive row of velocity stacks, and double nose fins. Then followed a silver-painted Mangusta and, finally, a red Pantera. Placed behind the cars, along the wall, were various engines — some still on their display

De Tomaso was not satisfied to build racing cars and grand touring machines only. Featured on these pages is another of his creations – the Deauville, a high-priced, four-door luxury saloon. Introduced in 1970, it is still in the catalog today. Altogether, less than five hundred are thought to have been built. The styling is by Ghia. The engine is by Ford – the same unit used in the Pantera, but mounted up front, driving on the rear wheels. The Deauville has not been made available on the United States' market. De Tomaso was accused of copying the Jaguar XJ series, and while there are definite similarities, the Deauville has distinctive lines all its own. (Photographs by Winston S. Goodfellow.)

stands. I would have liked to study this collection in more detail; the castings and the chassis construction in particular. But, our guide was getting restless.

Down the line, we saw the second of a total of three Panteras on the premises. It was an awesome-looking silver-painted GT5, with a V-shaped rear wing and an impressive row of five driving lights on a hood-mounted rack. The front air dam had been modified and the lower section of the body painted a darker shade of silver. The car also had an attractive custom leather interior with red fabric inserts.

Farther down the line, we saw the third Pantera — also a GT5, but dark blue. A few overalled mechanics worked on the front end, while a civilian stood to the side.

The man turned out to be the future owner. He was down from Switzerland and had expected to take delivery that day, but there were a few final adjustments to be made; the tubing funneling air to the front brakes, for instance, had somehow not been installed. Among other personal preference requests, he had asked that the shift lever be cut off two inches. This too had somehow been overlooked.

He told us that it had taken the factory about three months to build the car, and that they usualy would wait for a handful of orders to accumulate before starting on a batch. This policy was probably the reason for the lack of cars at the particular time of our visit. During the assembly of his car, he had been down three or four times to check on its progress. He had picked his options with the utmost care; it was virtually a racing car, with oversized brakes, front-mounted oil cooler, roll-bar, external power switch and the Group 3 engine modifications, which he expected would give him 350 hp and a top speed of 165 mph. He had also ordered the same gearing that had been used on the Panteras competing at Le Mans.

Even though the car was set up for racing, he didn't plan to use it for that purpose; he had chosen the Group 5 package, with its spoilers, flares and skirts, for the looks; the power, he had chosen for his trips to Germany and the Autobahnen, as well as for the occasions when he wanted to join the Pantera Club at the Hockenheim circuit for club events. We made arrangements to talk more at Arnaldo's. Our guide was getting restless again.

Next on the tour we saw a couple of Longchamps, awaiting finishing touches. All the way in the back, on the other side of a divider wall we probably weren't

(continued on overleaf)

De Tomaso's Group 4 racing car provided the initial inspiration for this awesome-looking showcar. The riveted-on fiberglass flares, as available from the factory, were used for starters. The rest was created by Hall Pantera of Bellflower, California. The many rows of louvers help improve airflow to both radiator and carburetor. Gotti wheels were chosen, and fitted with superwide P-7 Pirellis. Two-tone paint, pinstriping and black-powder-coated trim tops off the effect of this show favorite, here silhouetted against the ragged profile of a Long Beach oil refinery. The 1972 model, chassis number 3387, belongs to Tom Wilson of Cerritos, California.

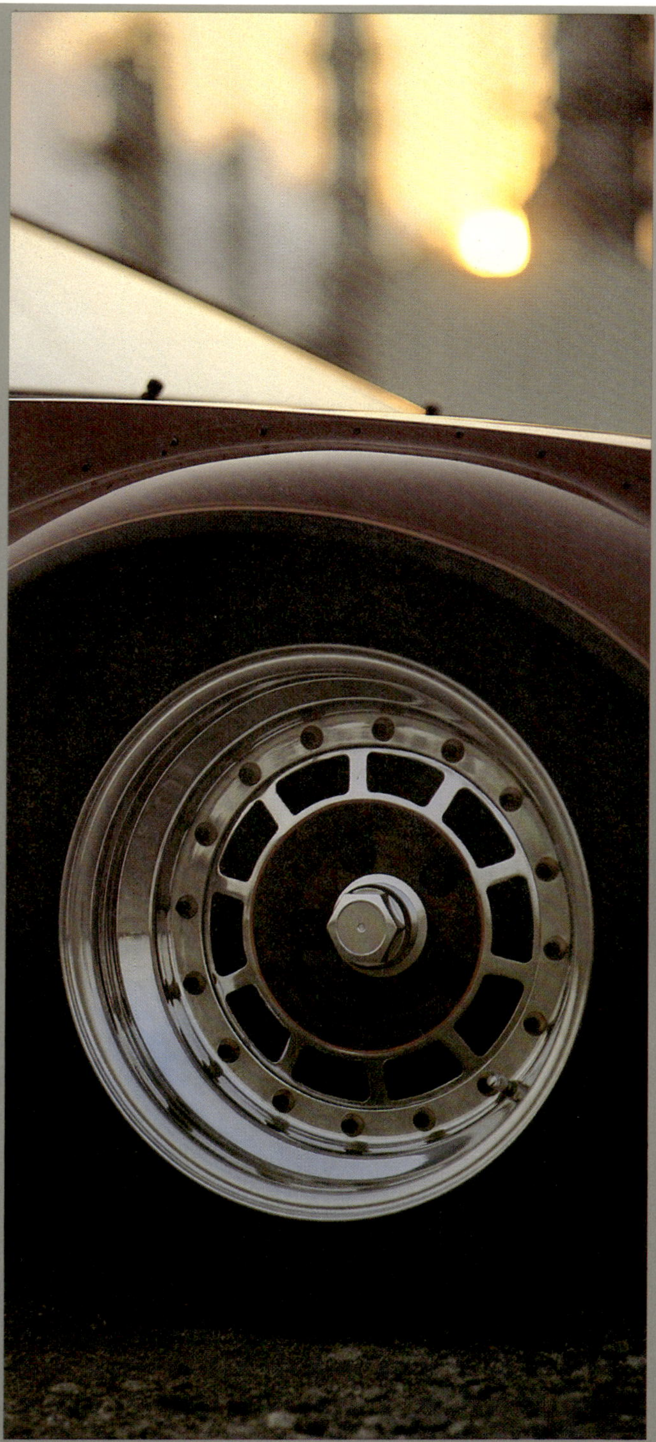

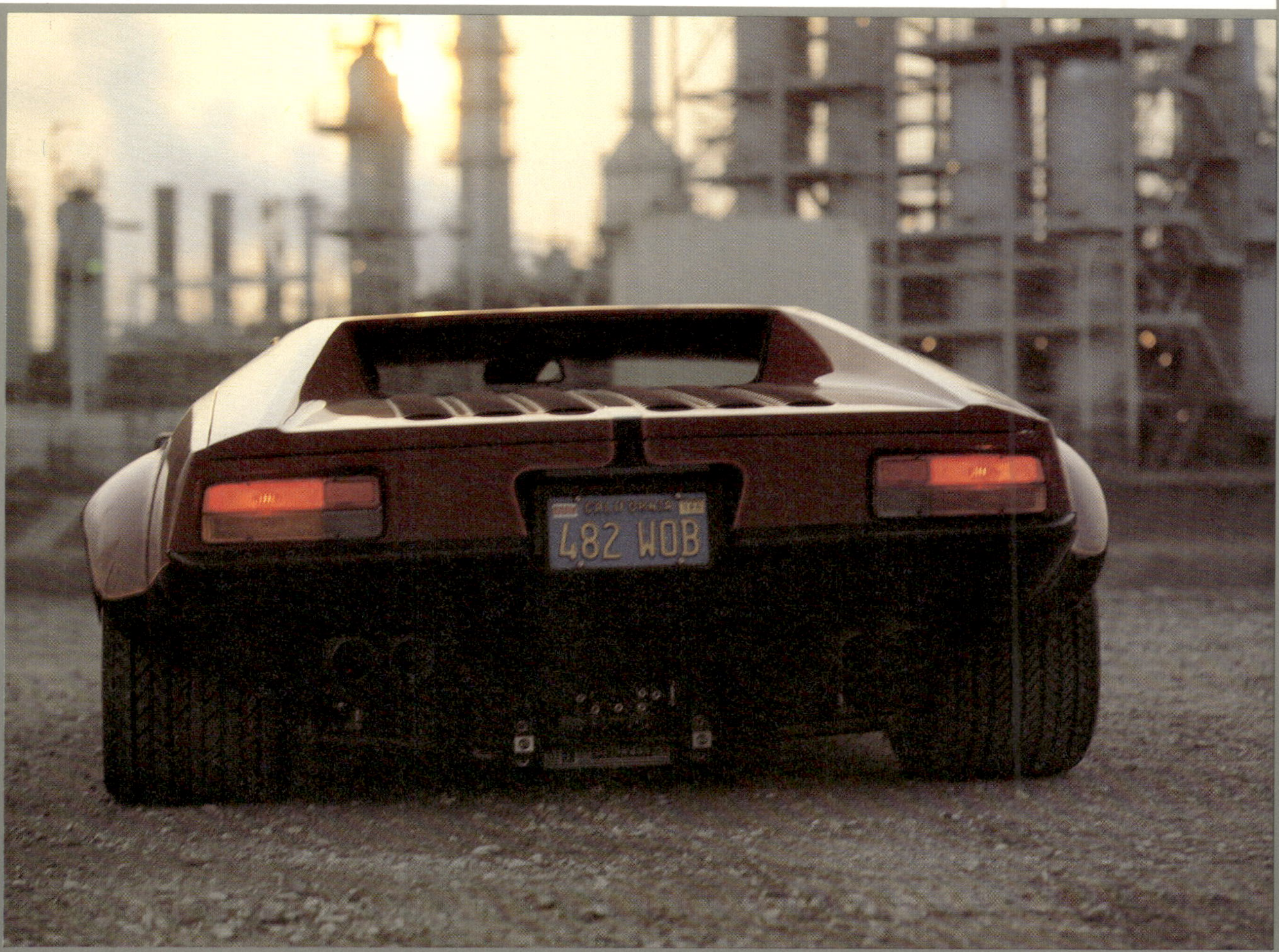
CALIFORNIA
482 WOB

meant to look behind, we caught a glimpse of a prototype car. It was the Maserati Biturbo! We realized, then, the probable cause for the picture black-out! The way back took us through a jungle of floor-to-ceiling parts shelves. Outside, we inquired about the third building, the low one with the blue doors. She told us it was where the engines were stored and tested. It was off-limits. But we expected that.

Upon our return to the office, we encouraged our guide to ask Mister Bertocchi to let us photograph the silver Pantera. We instructed her to tell him that we had spent a lot of time searching for a location, and that we had found one nearby. She gave us a look of total resignation, left with a deep sigh and returned almost immediately, reporting that the car belonged to a very private customer, and that it under no circumstances could be photographed.

Later that evening, at Arnaldo's, trying to sort things out, we came to the conclusion that the visit had been worthwhile after all. Although we had met our share of losers on this trip — and almost given up ourselves — we had fought a good fight. It wasn't a knock-out victory — but one on points — the result of methodical counter-punching. Our simple suggestion that the license plates of the silver Pantera be covered up, stubbornly submitted through our sweet and mild-mannered guide as a last desperate effort, had paid off, and she had returned, for the first time showing us what an attractive smile she had.

Ivano Cornia, the young sympathetic test driver, had driven the silver Pantera to the location. We had arrived just in time for that good late sun, and in spite of the icy wind that had made it necessary for me to warm up between every roll of film — Tomas had kept the BMW running and hot like a sauna — the pictures turned out to be some of my absolute favorites.

When our Swiss friend joined us at the table, we told him the story of our troubles. Sounds just like a perfectly ordinary visit to the factory, he said. That's the way things work here. It seems like a miracle, I know, but when you finally see the completed car, he said, there can be no doubt in your mind that they must be doing something right! We had to agree.

So if you are contemplating a trip to the factory, remember not to expect too much. And remember to stay at Arnaldo's in Rubiera. Upstairs, they have a few wonderfully comfortable rooms at very reasonable rates. Downstairs, they serve some of the best Italian cuisine this famous region offers. It's just what you need after that perfectly ordinary visit to the factory...

Featured here is another of the three models still available from De Tomaso Automobili – the Longchamp. The Ghia-styled, Ford-powered luxury sports car has comfortable 2+2 seating. It was introduced in 1972 and has been a consistent seller since. Total production is thought to exceed five hundred. Pictured above, part of De Tomaso's display at the 1980 Frankfurt Show. A convertible Longchamp obscures a Deauville. To the right, another view of the convertible, here with the top raised. The two pictures on the opposite page show the latest development of the Longchamp – the GTS. (Photographs courtesy of De Tomaso Automobili and Winston S. Goodfellow.)

HALL PANTERA GTS

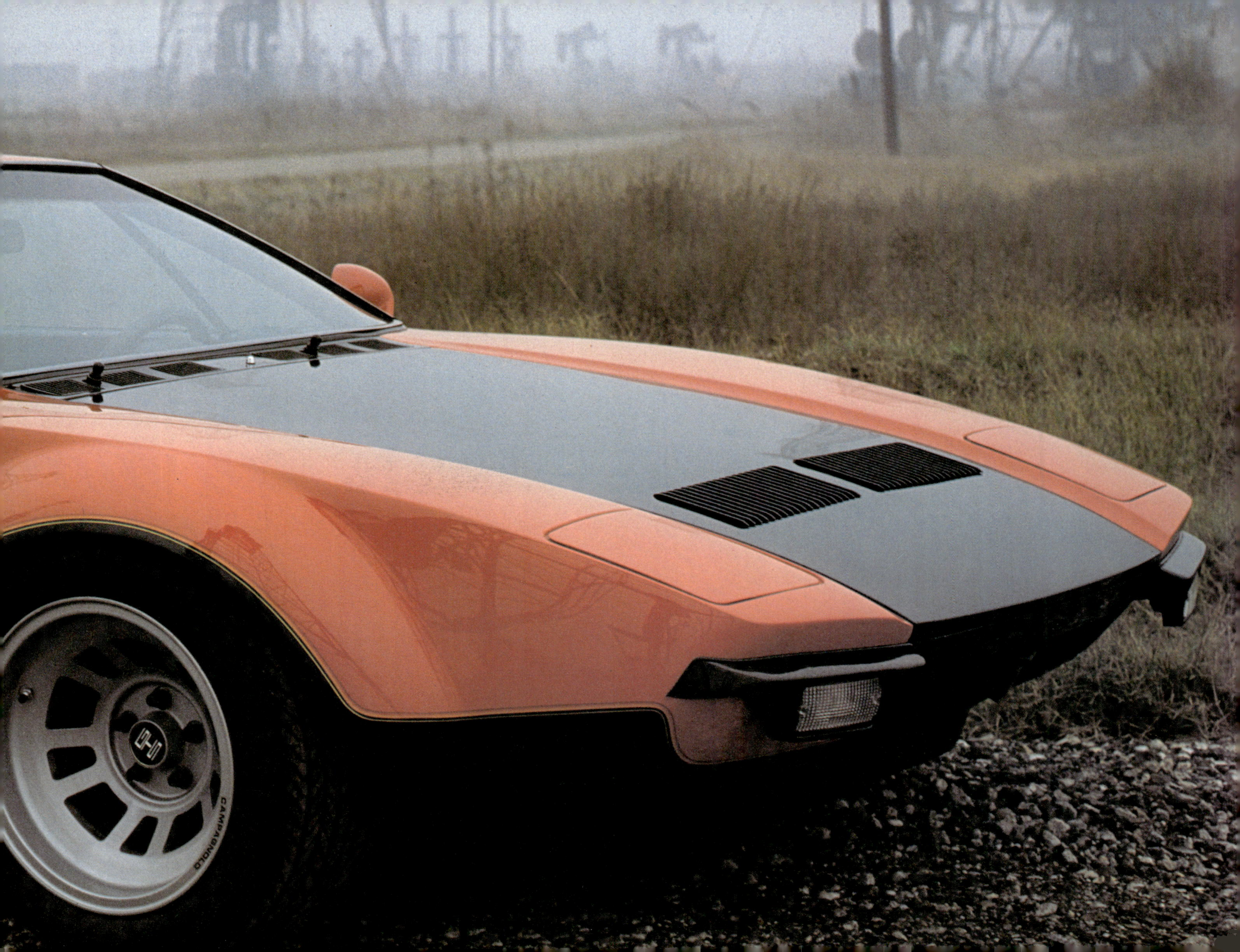
CAMPAGNOLO

Perfecting the Pantera

Part One

The Pantera was already from the beginning afflicted with a serious case of bad reputation. This could in part be traced to bad publicity. Bad, in the sense that the articles revealed the serious shortcomings of the Pantera. But also, bad, in the sense that some of the most influential magazines carried articles that painted too negative a picture, lacking in objectivity. One particular motor journalist, his article filling three pages, could find nearly nothing good to say about the Pantera. Maybe that was a result of looking too narrowly at the specific task of a road tester as he saw it — that of judging the workings of the machinery. But, maybe it also showed a lack of appreciation for the qualities of a car like the Pantera — for machinery is certainly not all that matters!

On the other hand, the bad reputation could also be traced to reports from owners of early cars. Their complaints were fully justified. De Tomaso had in fact left some of the work of the development engineers to the owners themselves — and to Ford. It went so far, that Ford found it necessary to establish a separate organization that had as a function to diagnose and correct these shortcomings. The early cars, every one of them, wherever they were in the country, had to be located and brought up to the new specifications.

Some observers point out that the owners of Panteras were often from a new category of enthusiasts — many of whom had never before owned or driven a car of this caliber and nature. These observers also point out that the Lincoln/Mercury dealers were not an ideal choice to handle sales and service, lacking both in enthusiasm and knowledge. Both of these factors seem to have compounded the problems.

Today, almost a decade later, most of the bad reputation is forgotten and the shortcomings forgiven. Sure, everyone knows they are there, or were there, but the Pantera is now appreciated for what it really is

When Gary Hall bought a Pantera in 1973, he soon found himself involved with the idea of improving and developing it. This involvement led to the establishment of Hall Pantera – a California based parts and accessory house. It also led to the building of Super Panteras – Panteras that have been totally restored and developed beyond factory specifications. On these pages, a few examples of what goes into a Super Pantera. Above, the ZF transmission, although brand new, is blueprinted and polished. Left, one car was fitted with nitrous-oxide. Right, another received four twin-choke Webers and Gurney Weslake Eagle heads. (Photographs courtesy Hall Pantera.)

— one of the most affordable, reliable, powerful and beautiful of the exotics. No longer is the focus on the bad aspects, but on the good.

There were some owners who saw all this from the beginning. One of these enthusiasts is Gary Hall. He bought a brand new Pantera in 1973 — chassis number 4200. He found that he enjoyed it so much that he decided it was a car he wanted to keep forever. Forever is a long time, and he knew he would need an ample supply of parts.

Just how serious Gary was about the parts situation manifested itself in 1975. After Ford had pulled out of the Pantera project and no more cars were imported, Bill Stroppe, whose organization had been responsible for bringing the cars up to specifications at port of entry in Long Beach, offered his entire stock of parts for sale. For a long time there were no takers; until Gary one day happened to find out that they were available. He bought everything; lock, stock and barrel or more accurately, for example: lower front grilles, door skins, windshields, light bezels, headlight buckets, axles, brake systems, wheels — everything! Gary had sold his own business in 1974, figuring on an early retirement; he wanted more time to play with the cars in his collection. Instead, the avocation turned into a vocation!

"Buying those parts was the smartest thing I ever did!" Gary tells me. We are in the inner sanctum — his private office. It is located in the back of a building that combines as showroom, offices, shipping center and warehouse. Typically, the showroom does not have any windows; the people Gary wants to see, all know where to find him. He leans back in the chair as he talks, calm and collected in spite of the constant buzzing of the phones, their hold-buttons blinking; in spite of the apparent disorder of the surroundings, every available spot filled with papers and parts. He goes on, telling about how the business, to begin with, just evolved by itself. "My original intention was to make sure I had a lifetime supply of parts. I knew it was more than I could ever use myself, but I figured I would share with other Pantera owners. I began advertising locally, but as it turned out, the owners only bought parts to get themselves out of emergencies, not for insurance, as I had done. I realized it would take forever to get rid of those parts, so I began advertising nationally. The demand soared; soon I spent a lot of time filling orders and answering phones. I finally had to involve my entire family and find a place
(continued on overleaf)

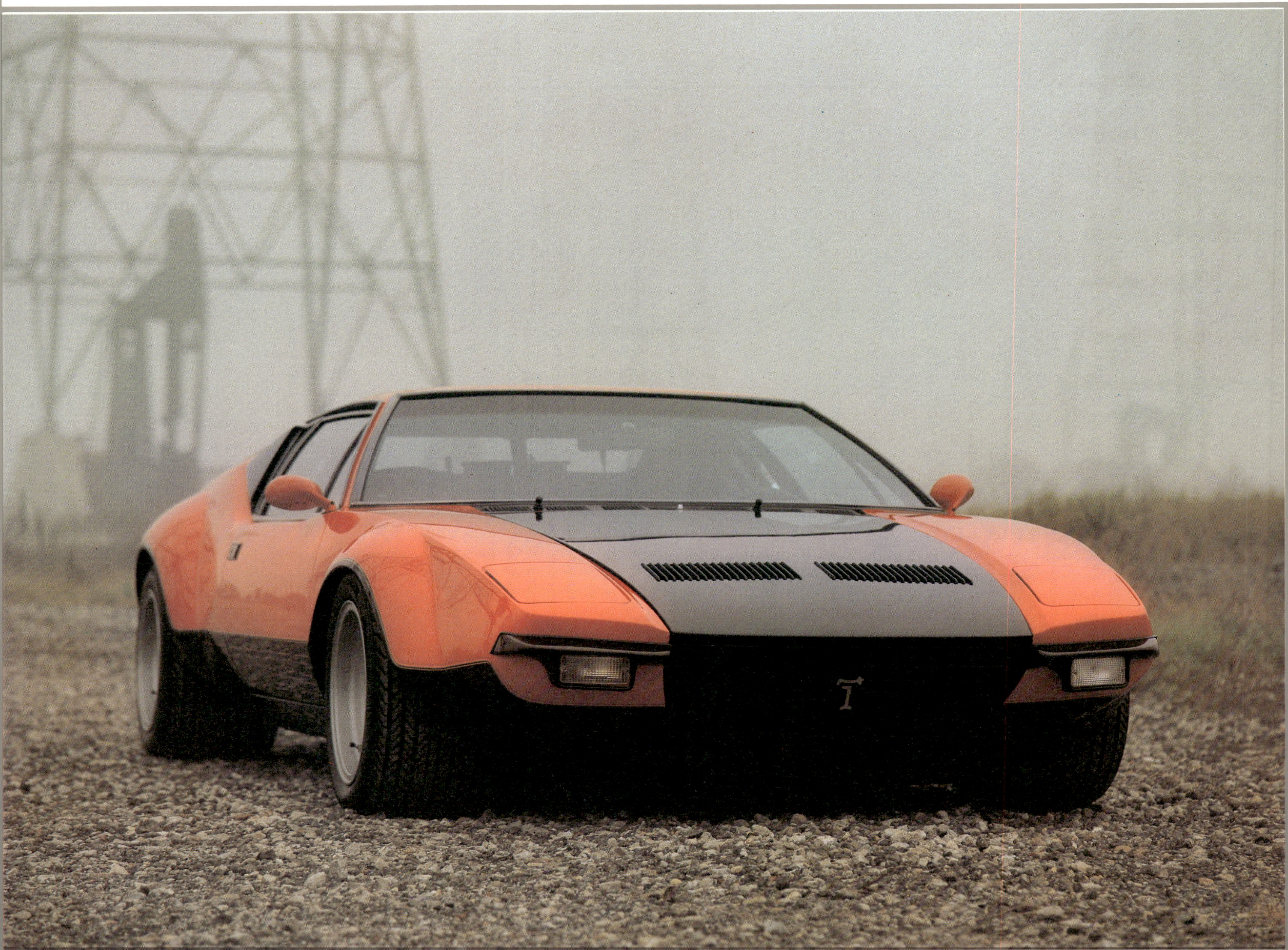

Oil towers and early morning coastal fog brings out the monster-like qualities of this custom-built Pantera. Hall Pantera of Bellflower, California, designed the welded-on steel flares that make this such a stunningly beautiful machine. What cannot be seen in a photograph, but must be heard, is one of the most exhilarating sounds one can ever extract from an engine; here created by the 180-degree exhaust system, also designed and built by Hall Pantera. The model year of this awesome machine is 1973. The chassis number is 4941.

of business. That's how Hall Pantera got started!"

As we talk more, between phone calls, I realize that it all actually began in 1937, back in Magnolia, Ohio, when Gary was only five years old. He can still vividly recall being taken for rides in his uncle's 1936 Ford V-8. He talks about that familiar rumble of the engine and about going to the circus in that Ford. After the war, when he turned sixteen, he bought his first car — a 1937 Ford Club Coupe.

"I spent more time working on it than driving it!" Gary says with a smile that recalls both the frustration and the enjoyment of those days.

In 1950, he bought his first new car — a Ford two-door sedan. Always Fords! Then came the long years of raising a family and building a business. During these years he was always faithful to Ford products, but it was first in 1970 that his car interest took more serious forms and he began collecting them, first specializing in Lincoln Continentals — of which he now has a complete line-up — then going on to other Special Interest Fords as well as to the high performance models, the Shelby Mustang, the Cobra, the GT 40. The latter, he is still looking for, but passively.

I ask Gary for his opinion of the much-talked-about shortcomings of the Pantera.

"Well," he says, "in the beginning it was popular to bad-mouth the Pantera. But, really, it wasn't all that bad. It was the best handling car I had ever driven. Very forgiving. In 1974, I drove my Pantera, totally original, in club track events, and scored the second best time of the bunch — and there were both Cobras and Ferraris among them!"

I ask about the overheating and the air conditioner that would never work well.

"There are improvements I think every Pantera owner should make. Basic ones. First. Fit Pirelli P7s! Get rid of that radial roll. The P7s improve ride and handling dramatically. Next. He should fit high-flow fan motors. Next. He should install a rotary air compressor for the air-conditioning unit. It gets rid of that crazy rumbling at 2000 rpm in fifth. Next. Change the electric window switches! I use Bosch. Next. Install a heater shut-off valve. It prevents heat from entering the cockpit and interfering with the air conditioner. As a last thing, I would suggest that he change the master brake cylinder to one that is rebuildable. Those are the basic things!"

"And now he has a good car?" I ask.

"Now he has a damned good car!" Gary says, never missing an opportunity to plug the Pantera.

Gary Hall was a Ford-man long before the Pantera arrived on the scene. Above, he is seen with one of his trophy-winning Lincoln Continentals. The rest of the pictures on this spread show a few of the components developed by Gary in the process of building Super Panteras. Left, quick-fill gas tank filler of cast aluminum. Opposite page, top, louvered radiator cover and hood vent kit. Far right, heavy duty swag bar bracket, milled from a solid billet of aluminum. Bottom, Ultra Wheels with anodized centers and correct off-set. Far right, dashboard insert of anodized aluminum. (Photographs courtesy Hall Pantera.)

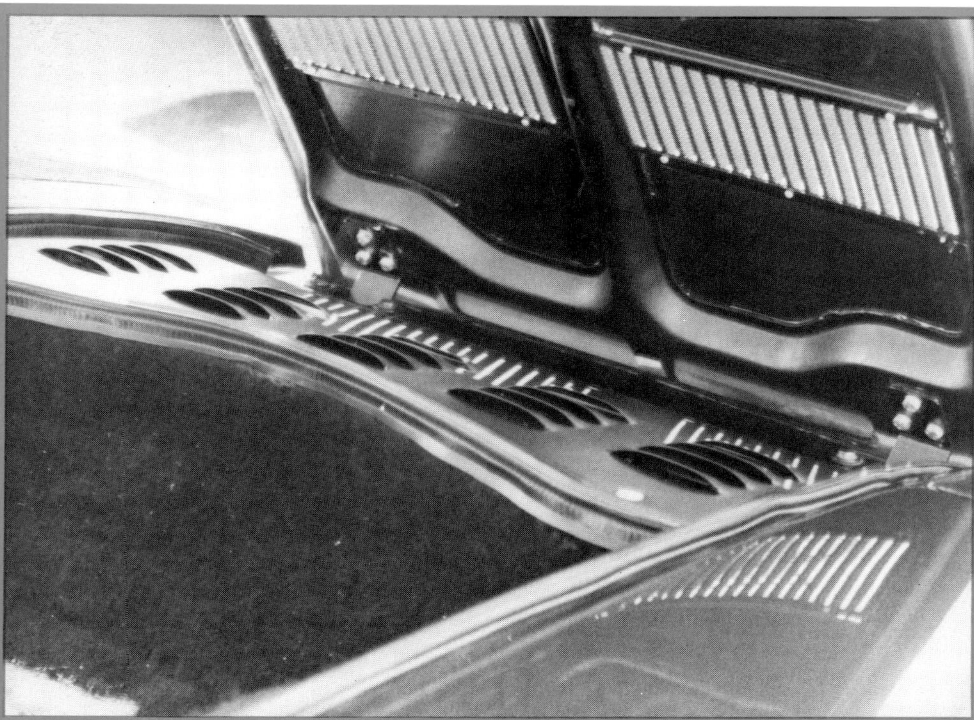

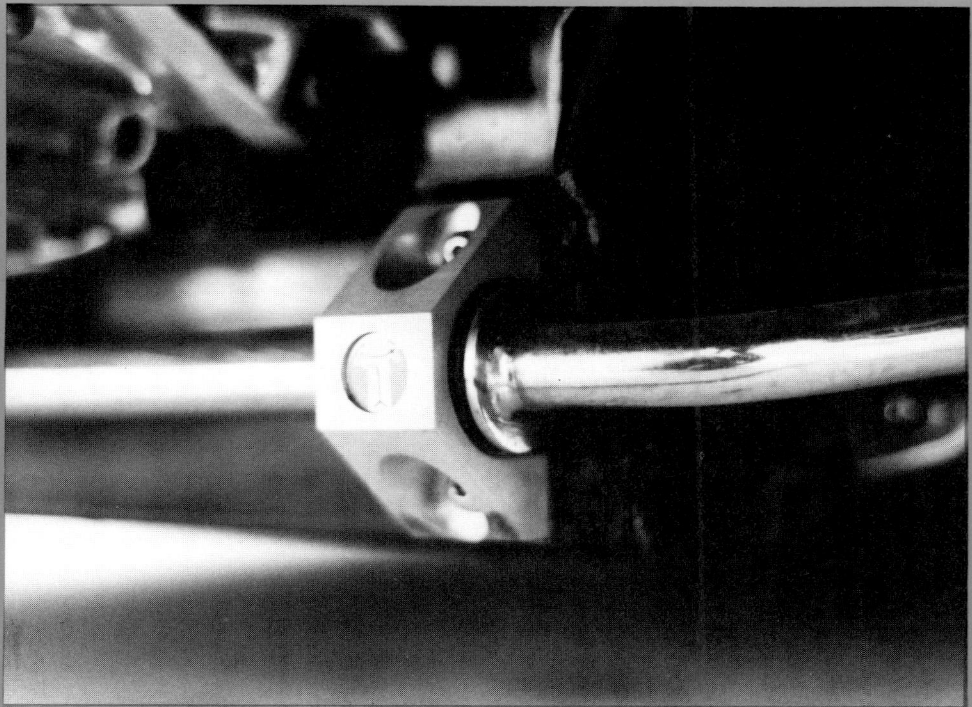

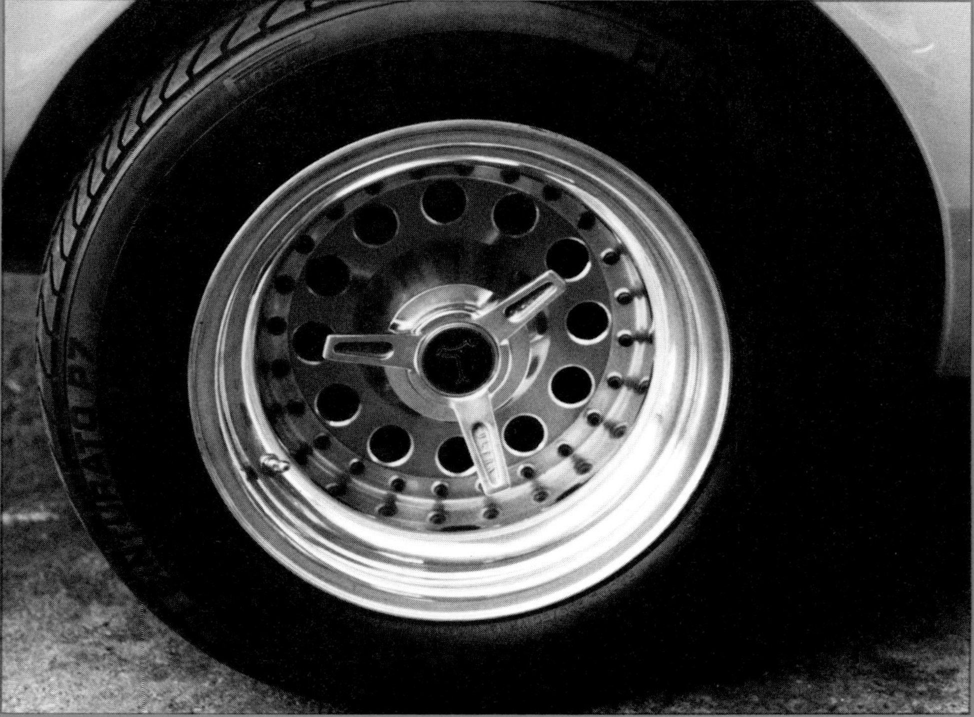

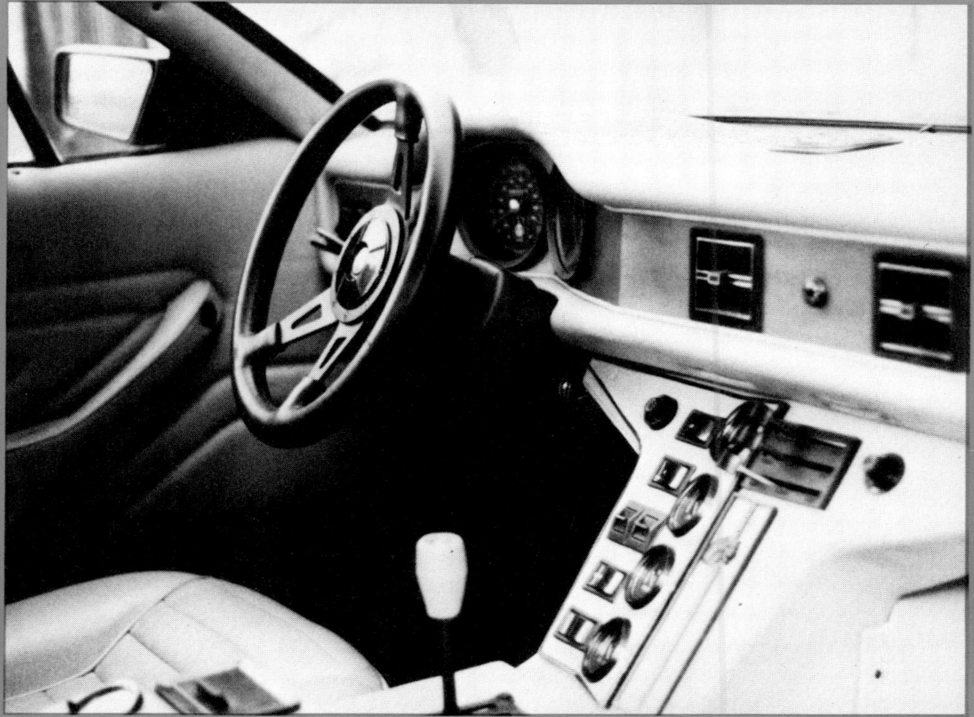

HALL SUPER PANTERA

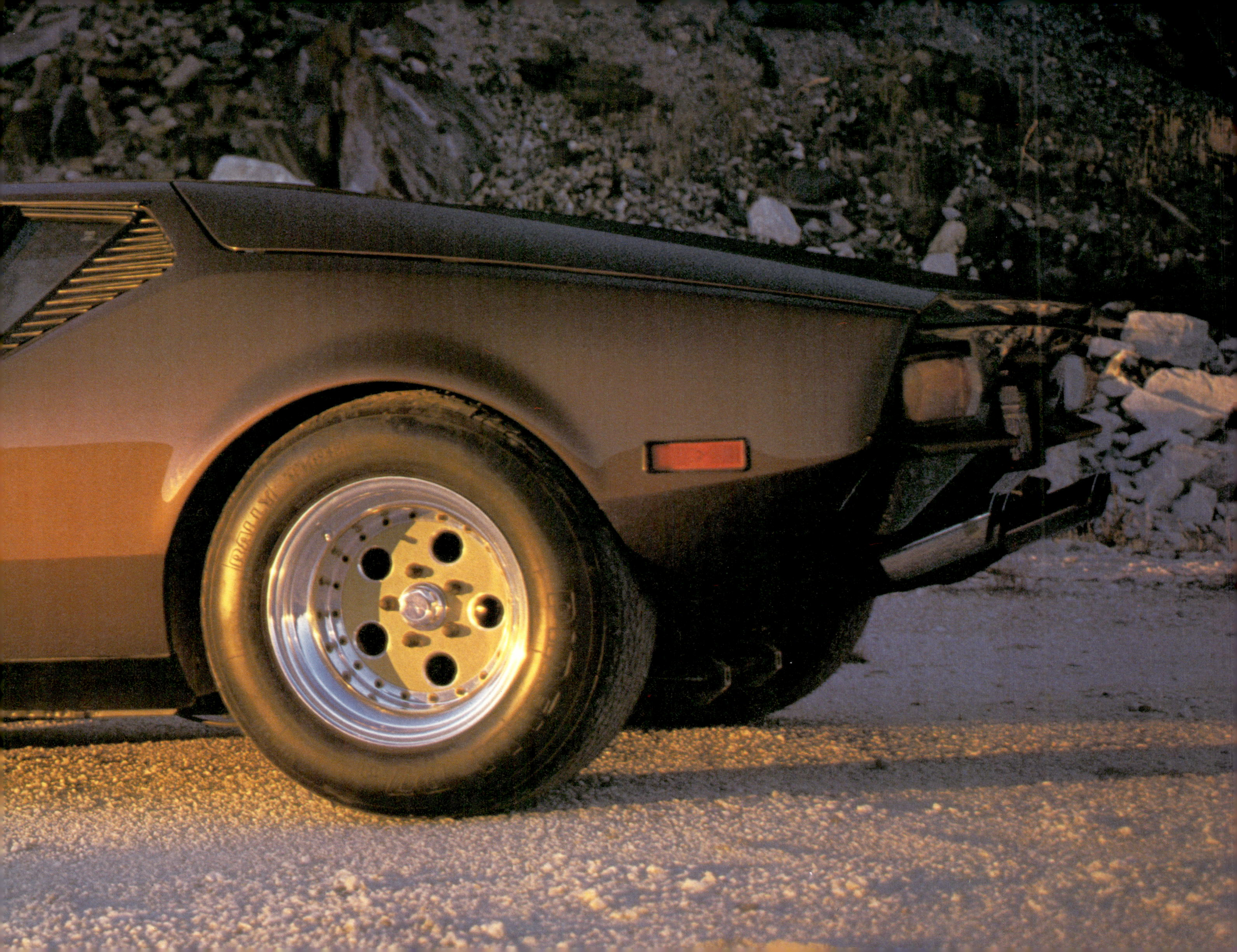

Perfecting the Pantera

Part Two

Gary Hall is on the phone with a customer calling from Japan. I pick up a stock Pantera hub-carrier of cast iron, comparing it to Hall Pantera's aluminum casting. Gary is off the phone now.

"You haven't been satisfied with just making basic improvement to the Pantera, have you?" I ask, weighing the two parts in my hands.

"Correct. I'm attempting to take the stock Pantera and turn it into the ultimate GT car — money no object! That applies to appearance, performance and reliability. The idea has evolved over many years. By now, I have built a dozen Super Panteras."

"Could you give me a brief description of what a Super Pantera is?" I ask, readying my pen.

"I'll try!" Gary says with a smile that means it is going to be difficult to skip those small details. "We have two in the works. Each one will take about one year to complete. In the process of building Super Panteras, we have bought an upholstery shop, become partners in an engine machine shop as well as a body and paint shop. We also have excellent contact with the best craftsmen in the area, relying on them for the things we can't handle ourselves

"Okay. That's a brief background. Now a brief description of a Super Pantera: We start with a structurally sound car, one with no rust, one that hasn't been hit or butchered. We dismantle it completely, down to the bare chassis. We then dip it to remove the old paint, leaving it in the tank for a week.

"After that, we re-weld all the old welds to strengthen the chassis and improve its rigidity. Then we grind the welds for smooth appearance. We go on to melt out the old lead from between body panels, afterwards filling these joints with new lead.

"Then we get down to metal finishing the car. This means that we align doors and lids. They must fit perfectly. We also sharpen edges and smooth surfaces.

This process can take up to six weeks. It's done the old-fashioned way — the only way — and it's very hard to find people who can do it right anymore.

"In the meantime, our upholstery shop is working on the interior. We use Connolly leather and it takes five hides. We do it either according to the original pattern, or according to the new style found in the latest factory Panteras. We use the stock seats, but they're built up and improved. By the way, during the re-welding process we also lower the floor pans two inches to provide more room in the cabin.

"In the meantime, our machine shop is working on the engine. Well, it's not the same engine anymore. We start with an Australian block, which is cast in a better type of metal and with thicker walls. It's fifty-five pounds heavier, but on the other hand, it can handle almost any increase of horsepower. We use a brand new block. Ford has just begun manufacturing them again. We use the stock crankshaft. We micro polish it. The oil holes are chamfered, the rods shot peened. The pistons are a forged competition version and give the engine a 9.0:1. compression. We use a special cam, manufactured to our own specifications. We use hydraulic lifters. The head is the stock Cleveland, but we give it a three-angle valve job. We use the best quality valve springs, aluminum roller rockers and chrome-moly push rods. The whole thing is topped off with aluminum valve covers, also manufactured to our specifications. We fit a high-flow oil pump and a ten-quart-capacity oil pan. We use an aluminum, by Edelbrock. The carburetor is by Holley and has center pivot float bowls. The fuel pump is also by Holley. The air cleaner is a cast aluminum, manufactured to our specifications. By the way, the flywheel is also changed to one of aluminum, which gives a quicker throttle response. All water and fuel lines are of braided steel with aircraft-type fittings. All bolts — in the entire car — have stainless steel socket heads. Two thousand dollars worth of them!

Pictured to the left and on top of this page, The GT4 – a 1972 racing version developed by De Tomaso. It was made available to private drivers, but was also campaigned by the factory – without notable success. Notice the racing filler cap, the sliding side windows, the riveted-on flares and the lack of bumpers. The lids, front and rear, were both of aluminum. Above and right, an example of De Tomaso's post-Ford production. It is difficult to classify as far as model description. It does carry the GTS decal, but does not have the flares. Notice that it is fitted with the Goodyear Arrivas and has the post-1974 hood vents. (Photographs courtesy De Tomaso Automobili.)

"Back to the body. It's primed and blocked — up to four times. We let all primer dry for at least ten days. Now we're ready to paint! We use acrylic enamel for toughness and long life. It takes about four gallons. That way there's enough of a layer to be able to eliminate any imperfections. We let it dry for six weeks before the final color sanding and hand polishing takes place. The engine bay, by the way, and the entire under carriage is treated with Body Schultz and is

(continued on overleaf)

When Gary Hall first became involved with Panteras, he soon found himself improving them. After having rebuilt ten cars to his rigorous standards, and after having founded his own parts business in the process, he is now closer than ever to knowing what makes a perfect Pantera. His latest effort is shown on these pages. It is a 1974 model with chassis number 7074, now owned by Maralee McGill of Garden Grove, California. The wheels are of his own design. The original light-buckets have been replaced by new ones, also of his own design, allowing rectangular quartz lights to be used. This outstanding Super Pantera won its class at the 1981 Newport Beach Concourse.

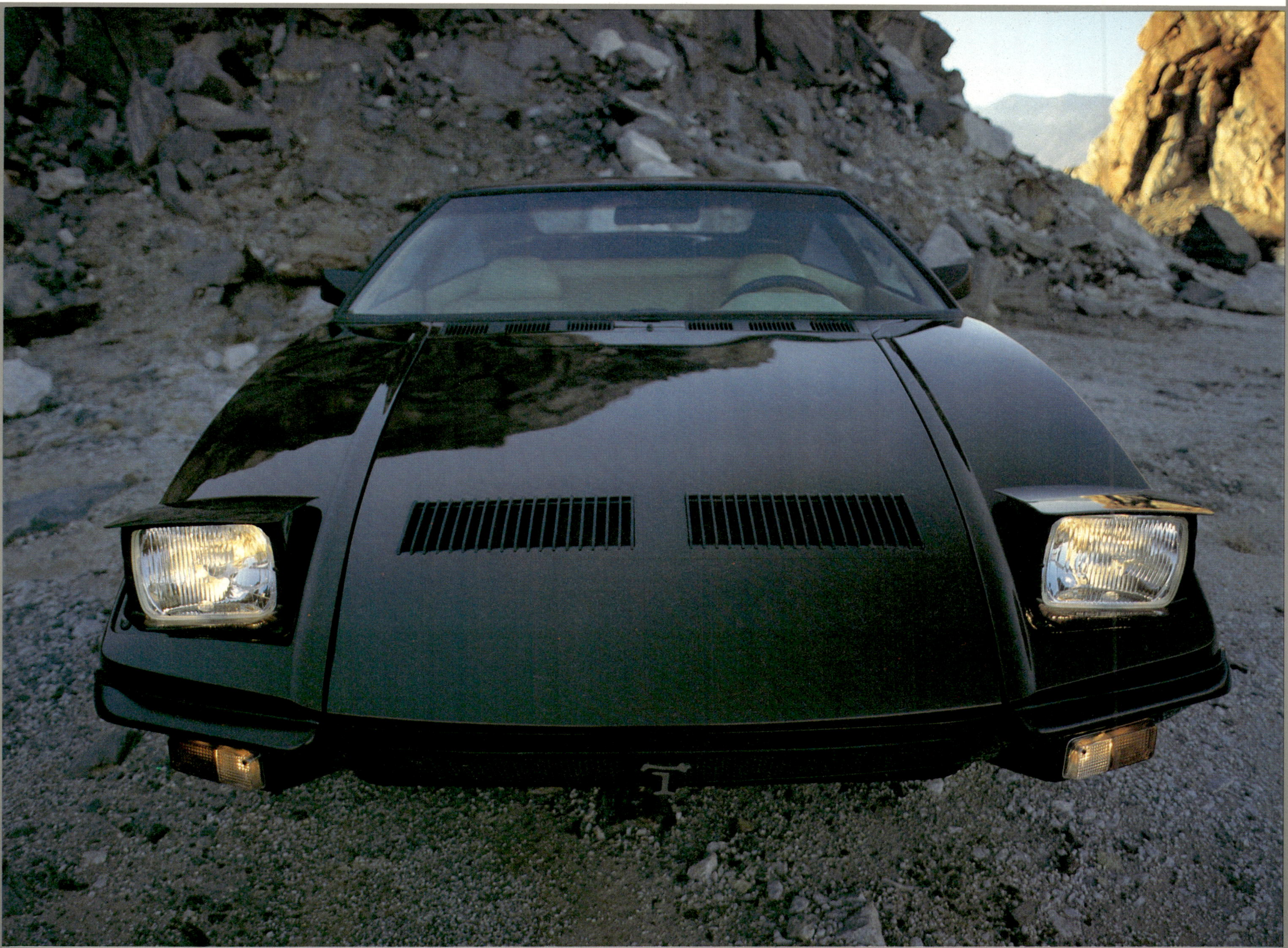

sealed with black enamel. We have by now also installed new headlight buckets specially designed by us to hold square halogen quartz lights. All exterior trim is powder coated a matte black.

"The suspension components are reinforced and powder coated with gloss black. Right now we're manufacturing a new suspension system of 4130 chrome-moly tubing. Mountings will be stock. The stock castings are duplicated in aluminum to save weight. We already manufacture our own wheels. We call them Ultra Wheels. They consist of four elements: the two halves of spun aluminum rims, polished and drilled, the machined center, anodized in appropriate color and drilled, and the spun aluminum hub. They're lighter and stronger than the stock wheels, allow for the correct off-set, and can be manufactured in any combination of width and size. We're also manufacturing our own brake system with fully ventilated, enlarged discs and aluminum calipers. With the stock brakes, by the way, it takes 140 feet to stop from 60 mph. With our brakes it takes 100 feet. We install shorter springs, supplied to our specifications. That's also the case with the gas/fluid shocks fully adjustable. Right now we're improving the suspension. We're experimenting with a design that will prevent alignment settings in the front suspension from changing.

"We musn't forget the cooling system. We install a new radiator that has seven rows of water tubes instead of the four in the stock radiator. We also cut vents in the hood for better heat dissipation. Ten bladed fans are also installed. We now have a fifty percent increased air-flow and hundred percent greater cooling capacity.

"That's about all. I'm sure I've forgotten some important details, but you wanted it to the point!"

"Two more questions!" I say, looking at the row of blinking hold buttons on Gary's phones. "First: Why?"

"We're all striving for the ultimate, aren't we? But, the goal here isn't only to construct the ultimate GT, nor to sell Super Panteras, but to develop parts and components that allow the enthusiast to make of his Pantera whatever he fancies: all stock, perfect show car, hot street rod, ferocious racing car. Our catalog now includes over four hundred items, ranging from all the stock parts to all kinds of accessories to all the Super Pantera components."

"Second: How much?" I ask with the pen ready.

"Seventy-six thousand!" Gary says without blinking. But he must have seen me blink. He adds with an appeasing smile: "I told you: Money is no object!"

The original GTS provided inspiration for this Hall Super Pantera GTS. It has black front and rear hoods, super-wide De Tomaso racing wheels and wide flares to accommodate them. The flares take their shape from the riveted-on originals, but while they were fiberglass, these are steel and welded on. The interior, above, sports black leather, racing belts, and racing-style fire protection system. Right, the raised hood reveals an awesome sight – the 180 degree exhaust system gives the engine compartment the look of a snake pit. Left, the heat produced by the system needs six rows of hood-louvres to escape. (Photographs by the author.)

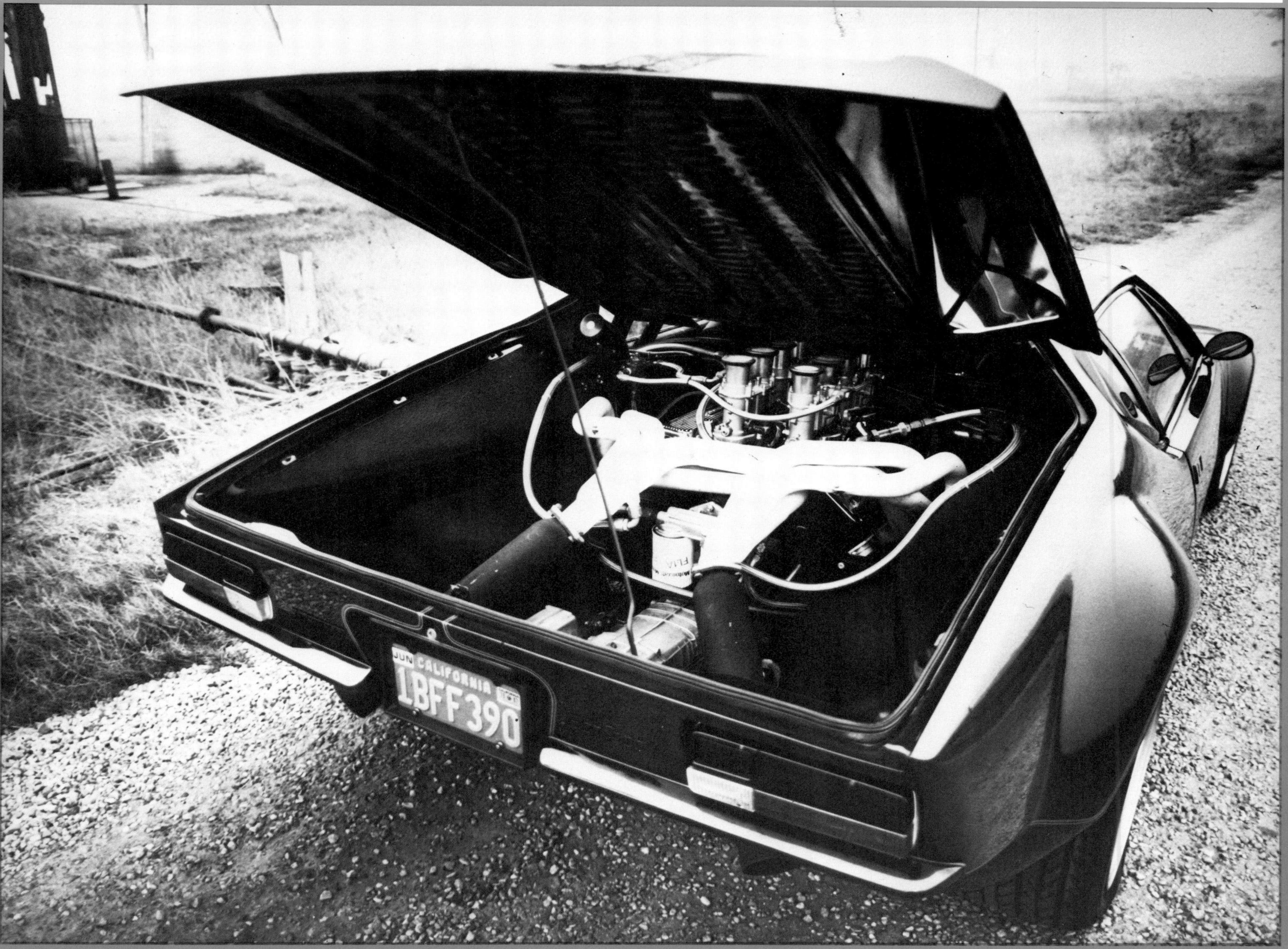
JUN CALIFORNIA
1BFF390

PANTERA TWIN TURBO

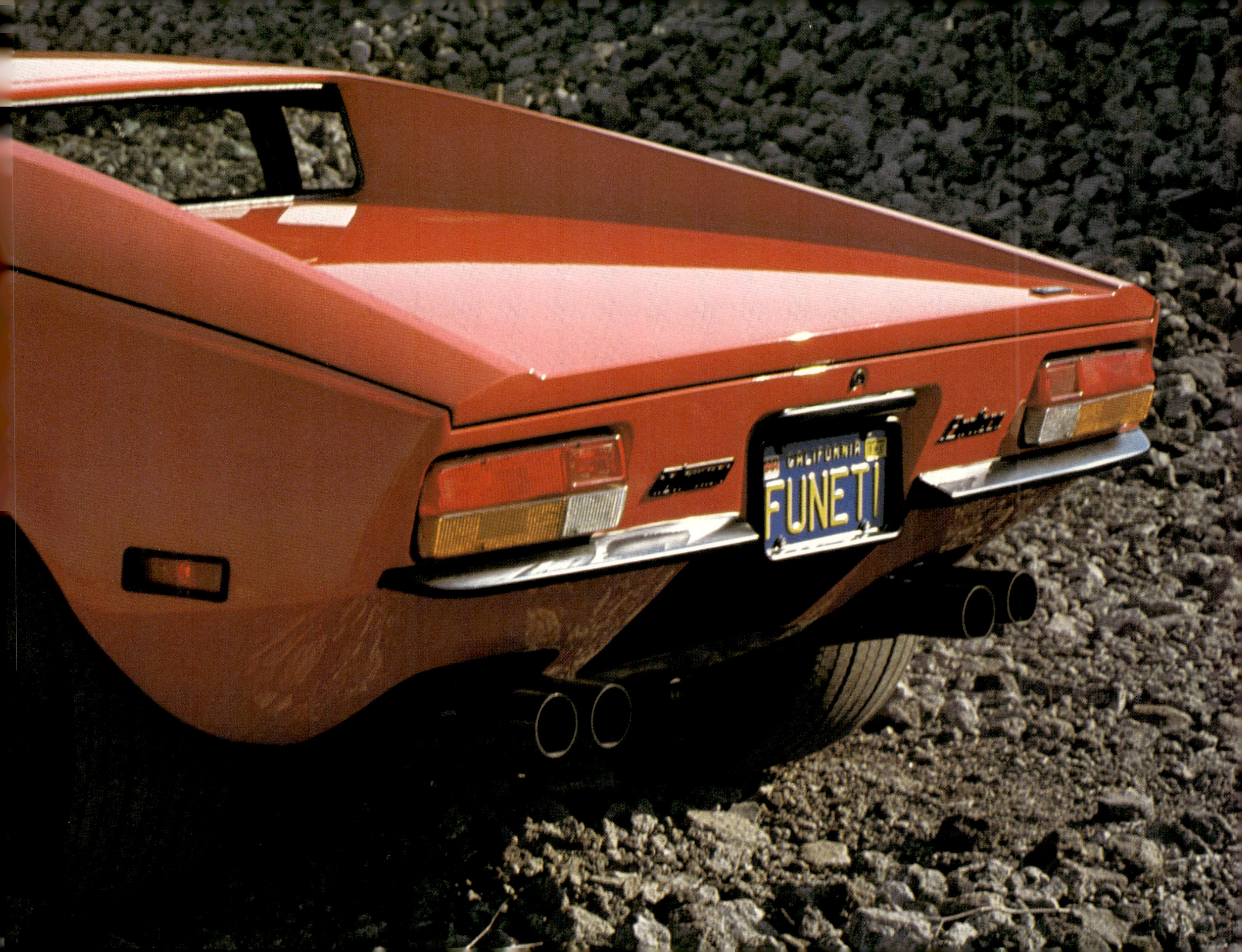

CALIFORNIA
FUNETI

Retiring a Show Winner

The red Pantera is rolling down the streets of Irvine, California, at a slow, deliberately restrained pace. The big engine is rumbling behind us, sounding subdued and seemingly dull and submissive. Owner Dennis Fugnetti is behind the controls. I am in the passenger seat, partly engaged in trying to find a position where my knees are not cutting into the lower edge of the dashboard, partly occupied with admiring the flawless appearance of the interior. From this inspection alone, it is evident why this Pantera is the most consistent winner at the Newport Beach Concours.

The sky is overcast. But there is no risk of rain. If there had been, and Dennis had been his old self, he would have raced back to the garage.

"I'm never going to show it again!" he says with determination. No! Now I'm going to drive it!"

The Pantera rolls on, keeping up that slow, deceivingly passive pace. I am finally accepting the fact that there is not adequate room for my legs. I am looking around some more. I am looking at the front end of the car, just barely visible above the lower edge of the deeply slanted windshield, showing a red shining surface that bounces sensually in synchronization with the irregularities of the road surface. I am looking behind me, through the glass of the rear window. I can see most of the twin turbo system; the finned airbox in the middle, the thick black porcelainized pipes, the aircraft-type fittings anodized red, the two turbine housings, one on each side of the airbox, wrapped in asbestos to keep the heat in.

Dennis is turning south now, away from the populated areas of Irvine. We are on a narrow road, lined with tall palm trees, surrounded by orange groves. Suddenly, unexpectedly, Dennis floors it, and the Pantera takes off like a Lear jet. At first there is just the normal roar of the engine, then you begin to hear a whistling, whirring sound. You can just barely notice it above the sounds coming from the exhaust and the wind rushing by. There is no jerk or kick when the turbo cuts in. And virtually no lag. Instead there is a constant surge, unbelievably powerful. A surge that you can feel in your legs as the blood is left choking in

The photographs in this spread, show the before-and-after condition of Dennis Fugnetti's Pantera. To the right, top of the page: the car is disassembled, but still has the scars in the front fenders from its unfortunate run-in with a big truck. The picture to the left shows the chassis in the straightening-out and weld-strengthening stage. One-and-a-half year of faithful attention by Dennis brought about a magical transformation. The contrast is evident in the pictures above and to the lower right, taken after Dennis was awarded first place as the owner of "Best Pantera of Show" at the 1980 Newport Beach Concourse. (Photographs courtesy Dennis Fugnetti.)

the veins and arteries. I can see it all happen like the frozen frames in a movie: the palm trunks slamming by in a gray blur, the trees flying past in sheets of green, oranges falling to the ground as if the branches had been shaken by a hurricane-force wind, the tachometer needle running right up to 5000 rpm, the needle of the boost gauge fluttering betwen negative and positive vacuum, then shooting up high, staying high in the yellow field for a fraction of a second — showing ten to fifteen pounds of boost — back to negative vacuum, the tachometer needle swinging back too; all this when Dennis shifts. And every time he shifts I hear a clicking sound when the lever hits metal at the bottom of the plate. There is little time to look at the speedometer, but I caught a glimpse of the needle pointing at 110 mph. That was just before Dennis downshifted and stepped hard on the brake, coming to a stand-still in front of a stop sign with the engine idling as if nothing had happened, rumbling peacefully.

"I like turbocharging!" Dennis says. "It makes the car behave both like a lamb and a lion. My wife used to drive this car to work every day!"

Born in New York City, on Manhattan's Lower East Side — Mulberry Street, to be specific — which is a very rough neighborhood, Dennis Fugnetti acquired a desire and appreciation for all things beautiful and perfect. By high school, he had moved to Fullerton, California. His first car was a 289 Ranchero — an excellent choice for the dual purposes of street racing and surfboard transportation. He became known among his friends for burning clutches and bending rods — such were his driving habits. His new life in California was still not easy; if he wanted something, like parts for an engine rebuild, he had to work for it. So, in addition to school and homework, he held jobs both as a cook and, later, as a night chef. A Barracuda with stickshift replaced the Ranchero. Then, suddenly, came a wife and a Dodge van — and no more wild or exotic cars until many years later when the photographic studio he started with a friend in 1974 began to return their investment of hard work.

He bought the Pantera in 1976. He liked the way it looked — like a piece of art! He bought it for his wife — always a good reason for acquiring an exotic car. So, she drove the Pantera — he drove the van. On the weekends, however, the roles were reversed. Dennis had discovered the Pantera Owners Club, and began to take part in time trials.

(continued on overleaf)

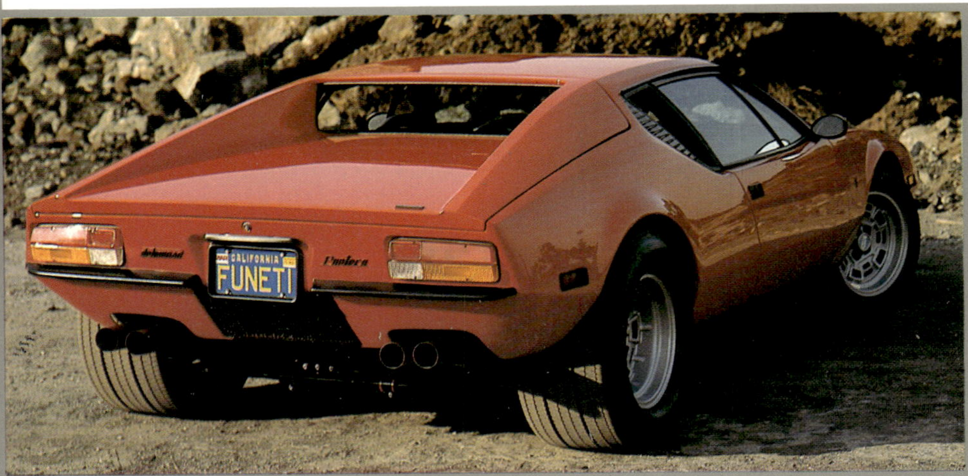
CALIFORNIA
FUNETI

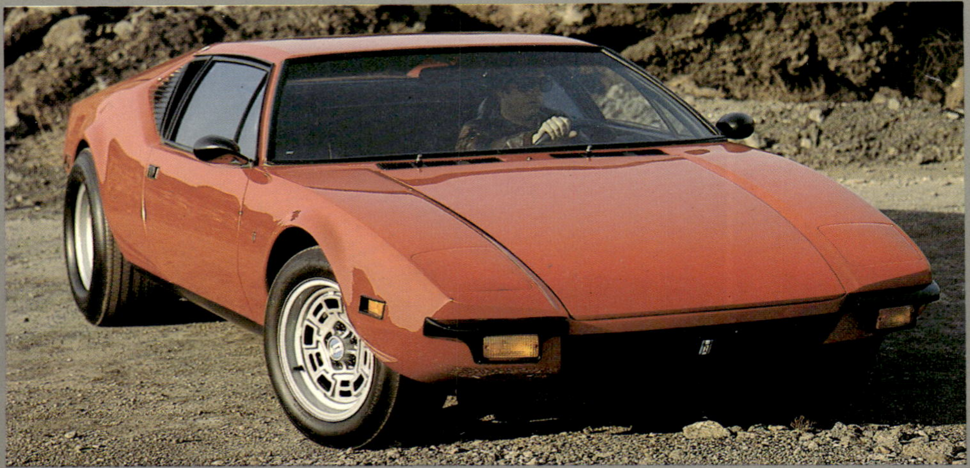

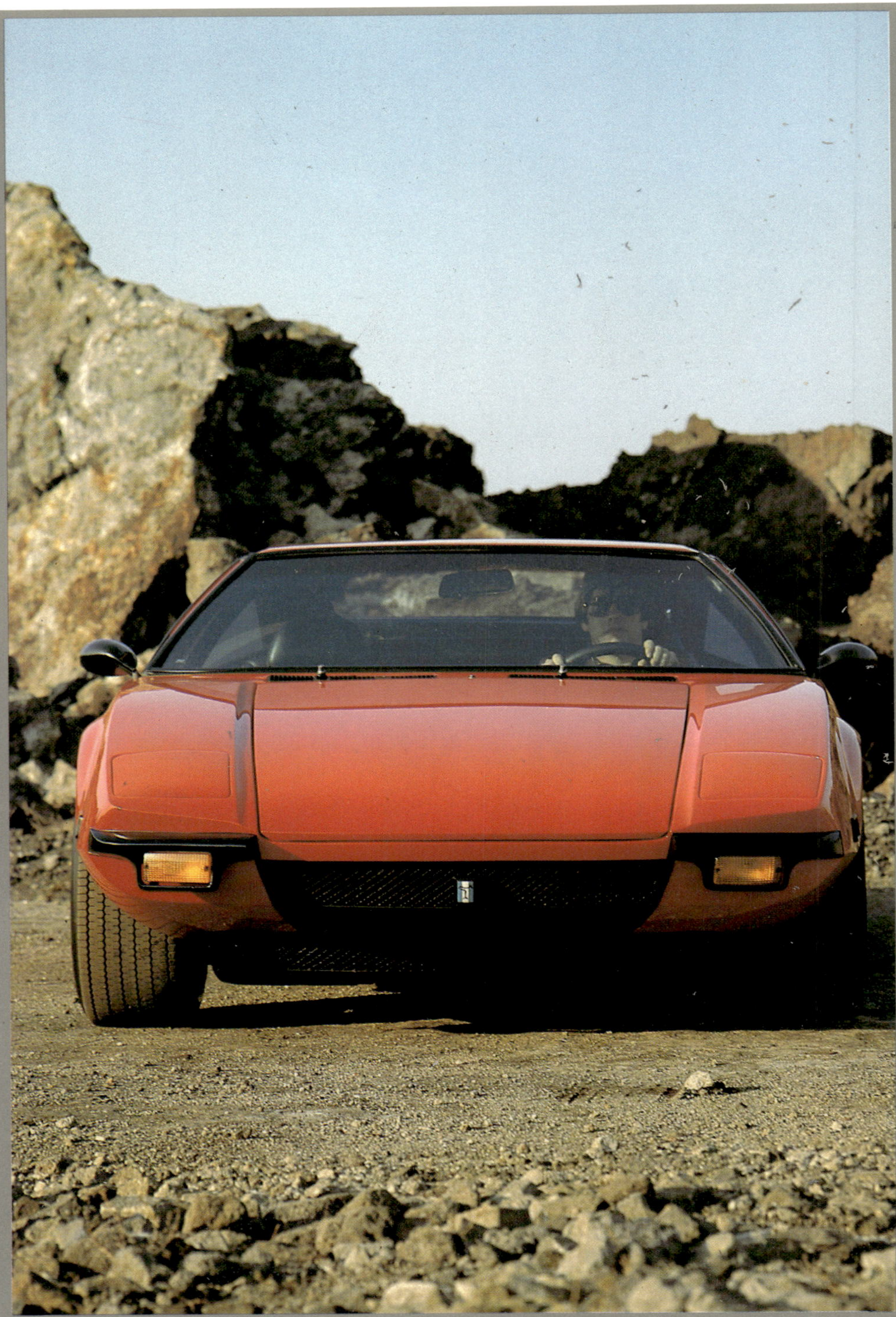

Black trim and fat tires are the only features to distinguish this from a perfectly original Pantera. It is first when you get behind the wheel, discovering the boost gauge, that you realize this is a turbo – twin turbo, no less! You are further removed from a standard Pantera as soon as you let out the clutch; as soon as you feel that tingling in your legs from the enormous pace of the acceleration. Owner Dennis Fugnetti of Anaheim, California, spent several years restoring this 1972 car, chassis number 2457. His first place win in the 1980, Newport Beach Concourse is proof of the outstanding condition of this car. The twin turbo is the final clincher in a marriage of beauty and power.

"The Pantera had five days of rest," Dennis says as he tells me the story, "and two days of hell!"

At that time he found that the engine was burning oil and that there were strange, unhealthy noises coming from it and he finally also bent a rod — again — so he decided it was time for a rebuild. With an eye on the need for increased power on the track, and the need to keep it smooth on the street, he decided to try turbocharging. It worked even better than expected — he captured and then defended the record at Riverside for two years, and his wife was still able to drive it back and forth to work.

"We jacked it up, changed to colder plugs, raced it, jacked it up, changed back to warmer plugs, and drove it home!" Dennis says with a reminiscing smile.

Now it was time for the next link in the chain of events. Waiting in line during the 1979 gas crunch, a big truck backed into the Pantera, chewing up the entire front end. This accident prompted Dennis to embark on a total restoration. Everything was taken apart, cleaned, stripped, welds smoothed, body defects lead-filled, sanded painted — all the necessary things. He worked on it every evening for one-and-a-half years. When he was done, he looked at it with pride, and thought it was nice enough to show. At that time, Steve Wilkinson, who had done the original turbocharging, looked at the engine, and felt the appearance could be much improved. He offered to do it for free, just to be able to show what he had in mind. At that time Steve was working out of his garage. Now, he has prospered, running his own business, specializing in total, ground-up restorations. This year's show winner was his work. But back to 1980! There was a lot of work to be done, and Steve and Dennis were up all night before that year's Newport Beach Concours. The next day, the car was chosen best Pantera of show! It was a winner of various categories and prizes during the following years as well, making it the winningest Pantera ever.

"What's your secret?" I asked Dennis as we park the car by the roadside and step outside to admire it.

"Attention to detail!" he answers. "And conservative taste. I've always felt that it was important not to destroy the original look of the car!"

"And now you are never going to show it again? You're going to drive it?" I ask.

"No! You're going to drive it!" he says with a smile.

And there it was again, the roar, the whistling, the surge, the flicking of the needles, the clicking from the shift lever, the blood choking in my legs...

In the picture above, Dennis Fugnetti pushes his twin turbocharged Pantera around a sweeping corner. He captured all the track records in the Pantera Owners Club speed events, defending them successfully for two years. In this picture, the car has still not undergone the the thorough restoration. To the left, one little tell-tale item inside the cockpit is the turbo boost gauge. It fits perfectly between the tachometer and speedometer pods. To the right, the source of all that power – the Ford Cleveland in all its twin turbocharged glory. The development of the system was the work of Steve Wilkinson. (Photographs courtesy Dennis Fugnetti).

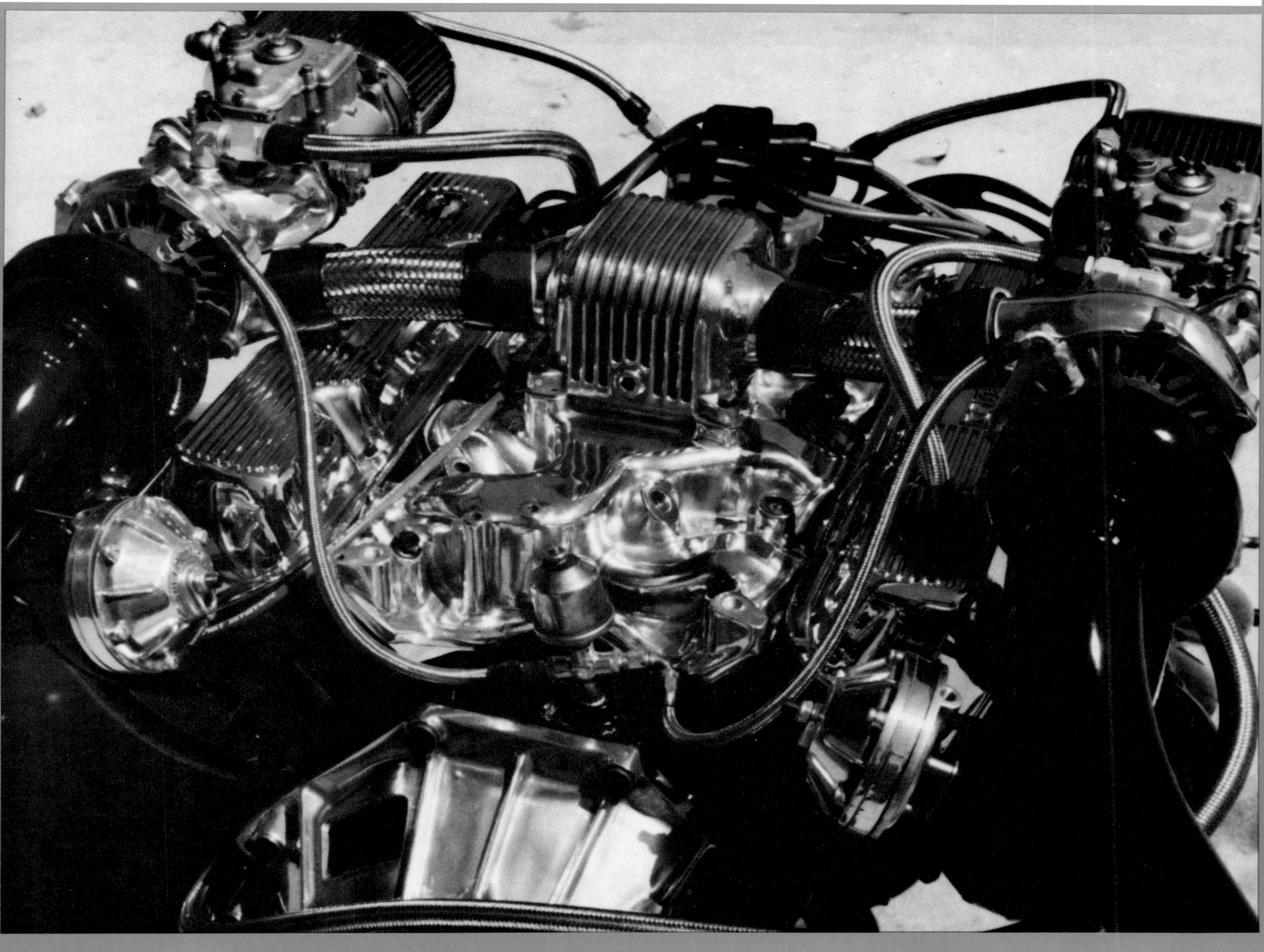

PANTERA RACING CAR

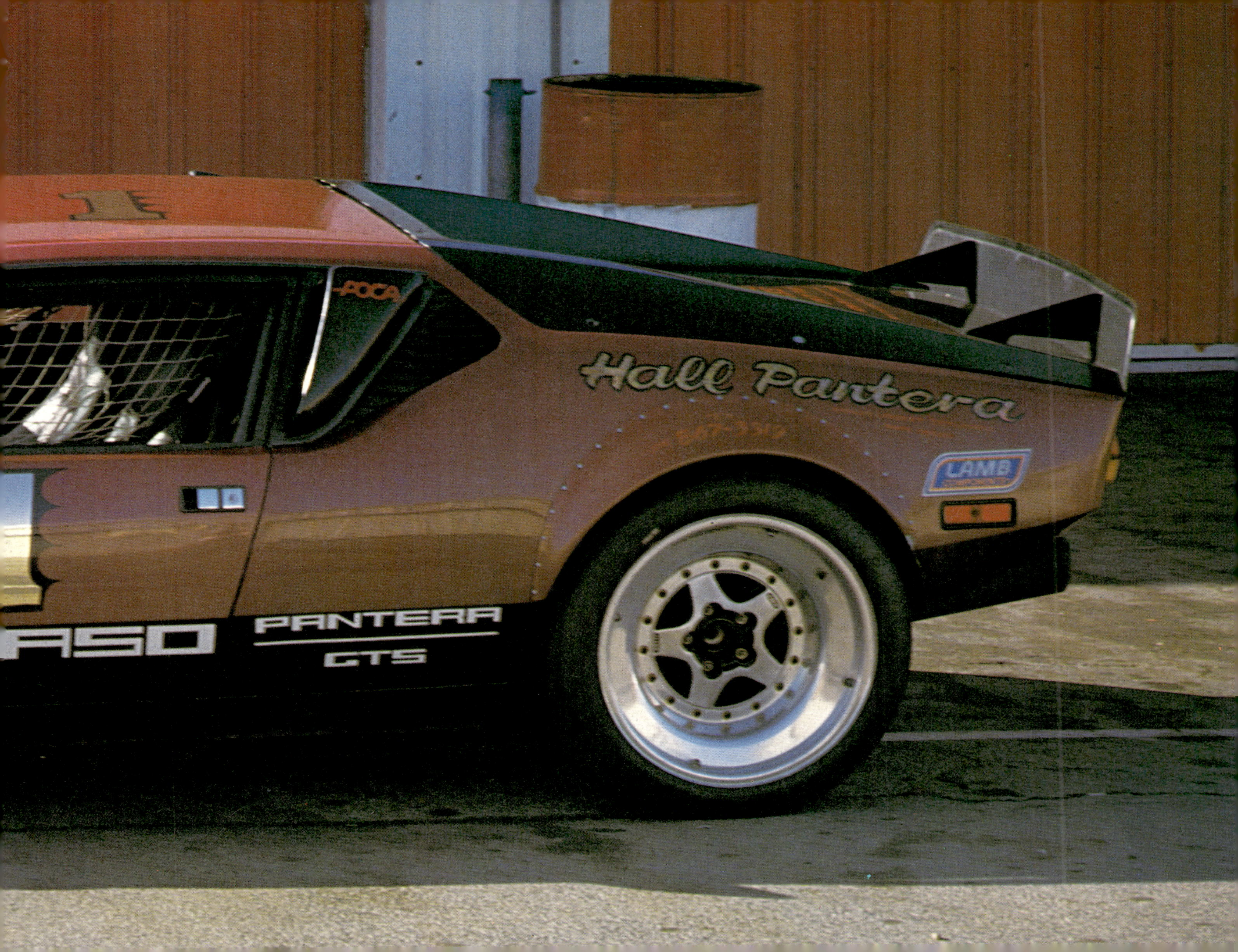
Hall Pantera
LAMB
PANTERA
GTS

Getting a Brake at Riverside

I feel anticipation. Even exhilaration. Also a little hesitation. What if something should go wrong? After all, these brakes are new. They have been made according to Gary's specifications by a small shop in Upland. Who knows how good they are? Who knows if he knows what he's doing? They have never been tested. This is the test!

I'm changing behind the trailer. Putting on the Nomex driving suit someone has handed me. I'm fumbling. A little too eager. In a hurry. Losing my balance. Jumping on one foot trying to regain it. The other foot is stuck at an awkward angle inside one of the legs of the suit.

The sky is dark above Riverside International Raceway. It looks like the rain could come any moment. If it does begin to rain, they'll close the track. Better hurry. I can hear the Pantera accelerate down the straight-away on the far side. The sound is exploding into a roar as the car comes shooting out from under the Champion Spark Plug Bridge. I can hear Gary shift into fifth. The engine runs all the way up to seven thousand before he brakes, going into Turn Nine. Better hurry. Gary is supposed to stop in the pits on the next lap. I'm to ride as passenger for three laps. That's all we have time for before they'll start timing. If it doesn't start raining before then! Better hurry. The suit is on. It's too small. Must look funny with a bit of bare leg showing between the suit and my out-of-place dress shoes.

The Pantera is going through Turn Nine now. I can hardly hear it. Coming from that direction, the sound is muffled by the garage buildings on the infield. I can hear it again when it shoots out of the turn. It sounds like a World War II fighter plane coming in for a landing. Instead of accelerating up the finish-line straight-away, the Pantera slows down and turns into the pit lane, still going pretty fast. It's big-wheeled and beautiful. Coming at you like that, with the nose down, it looks like a mean beast, ready to attack.

Gary is coming in. He probably thinks the rain is going to start any moment now. Or maybe there's something wrong with the brakes? Better hurry. I take a few running paces that get me up to the pit wall at the same time as the Pantera comes to a stop. I notice the big, nineteen-inch tall Gottis in the rear, wrapped in fourteen-inch wide Pirellis. Using those tall wheels, Gary can fit the lower A-arms inside the rims. That way he's able to put more rubber on the track than even De Tomaso found possible on his competition cars and still use the stock GTS flares, keeping the car narrow and aerodynamically more efficient. I notice the front spoiler. It's mounted much like the one on the GTS. But Gary's is wider and deeper, almost touching the track. I notice the rear spoiler, mounted on the tip of the deck lid, held in place by two brackets. Gary told me earlier that he had tried a wing and that he felt it was too dangerous. It was too effective. If you happened to end up going sideways, accidentally, you would suddenly lose all that pressure and it would compound your trouble, possibly causing you to spin out. I look at the rows of polished velocity stacks protruding through the deck, extending from the Webers. And I look at the black, four-inch exhaust pipes jutting out from under the car. Just then, Gary kicks the accelerator, cleaning the throats of the carburetors, sending waves of detonations through those pipes, sending them through as if there was an ammunition dump on fire in there, as if fifty-millimeter shells were exploding at the rate of one thousand a minute.

My hesitation is suddenly back. Wonder how those brakes are holding up? A voice inside tells me that this isn't the way to go. If you have to go, you should go while performing some heroic act. Another voice tells me that you have to go one of these days anyway. So, if you have to go, you might as well go this way. There are worse ways, you know! He died in a race car crash... I test the sound of that. But I'm not seriously hesitating. You don't change your mind when you already have the driving suit on and the car has stopped in front of you and the door is open and someone hands you a helmet. It's too late to change your mind then!

I bend down, squeezing into the passenger bucket,

The continued development of new components aimed at improving the Pantera is what intrigues Gary Hall. He takes the testing of these components very seriously. The racing car was developed for this purpose. In order to gain first-hand knowledge of their performance, he insists on driving the car himself, although only in friendly club-style competition. Above, he is ready to take off. Daughter Leslie wishes him good luck. The picture to the left seems to indicate that he needs it, but the broken leg was not the result of a car accident – he also rides motorcycles! Right, Bill Wysock assists Gary in preparing for some fast laps at Riverside. (Photographs courtesy Hall Pantera.)

pressing the helmet over my head, forcing it open wider to make it pass my ears. I'm fumbling with the chin strap. Someone takes care of it for me. Someone else reaches in to thread the harness over my shoulders. I reach for the waist-level safety belt, trying to buckle it. I'm fumbling with it too. Someone else does it for me. The car is trembling and the cockpit is reverberating with the sound of those detonations. My field of vision is limited from inside the helmet and I have to turn a little to see Gary in the driver's seat. He looks like an astronaut. I try to ask him how the brakes are working. But he can't hear me. Someone hands me a speedometer gauge. Just a gauge with a loose cable hanging from it! What am I going to do with it? Hold in in my lap? They hook up the loose end somewhere under the dashboard.

They're checking the tires now. What about checking the brakes? Will someone check the brakes? Apparently not. Well, if it's time to go, it's time to go! I look around inside the cockpit. It's gutted. Virtually nothing is left of the stock Pantera interior. The seats are Huntmasters from England. True racing buckets. The dash and the console are of aluminum, covered with vinyl. By the way, the doors and front and rear lids are also of aluminum, I remember Gary having told me. The steering wheel is the original, fat-rimmed Ferrero, used on the GTS. Behind the wheel, angled right toward the face of the driver, sits a tachometer. The shut-off can be dialed in. Gary has it set on 7200. Mounted on top of the tach, is a Pro-Lite. It monitors the oil pressure. Should it sink below thirty pounds, the light will come on, showing bright red just in the driver's field of vision. That's so he can kill the ignition at once, saving the engine from disintegrating. There are three gauges on the mid-section of the dash. The first monitors the water temperature. The second monitors the oil temperature. The third, the oil pressure. They're turned so that under normal conditions the needles will all point straight up. One quick glance will tell if something is wrong. On the console, between the seats, are rows of lights and toggle switches. The first, the green, is for the ignition. The second, the blue, is for the alternator. It can be disconnected under special circumstances during a race when some extra go is needed, freeing another ten horsepower. The third, the yellow, isn't connected. It's there for the eventual use of nitrous oxide. The fourth, the red, controls the brake lights. This feature can be

(continued on overleaf)

Brute Power" is the slogan painted on the hood of Gary Hall's racing Pantera – and that is no exaggeration! This car was the first ever to break the two-minute lap time barrier during time trials on the road racing section of Ontario Motor Speedway. A Ferrari 512 LeMans Boxer and a McLaren Mark 6 were left behind. One would have wished for this kind of thing in the early seventies when the Pantera badly needed racing successes. The car was a 1974 GTS, chassis number 6880, before being turned into Gary's development car – the one he uses to test new products before they are being marketed through his parts and accessory firm, Hall Pantera.

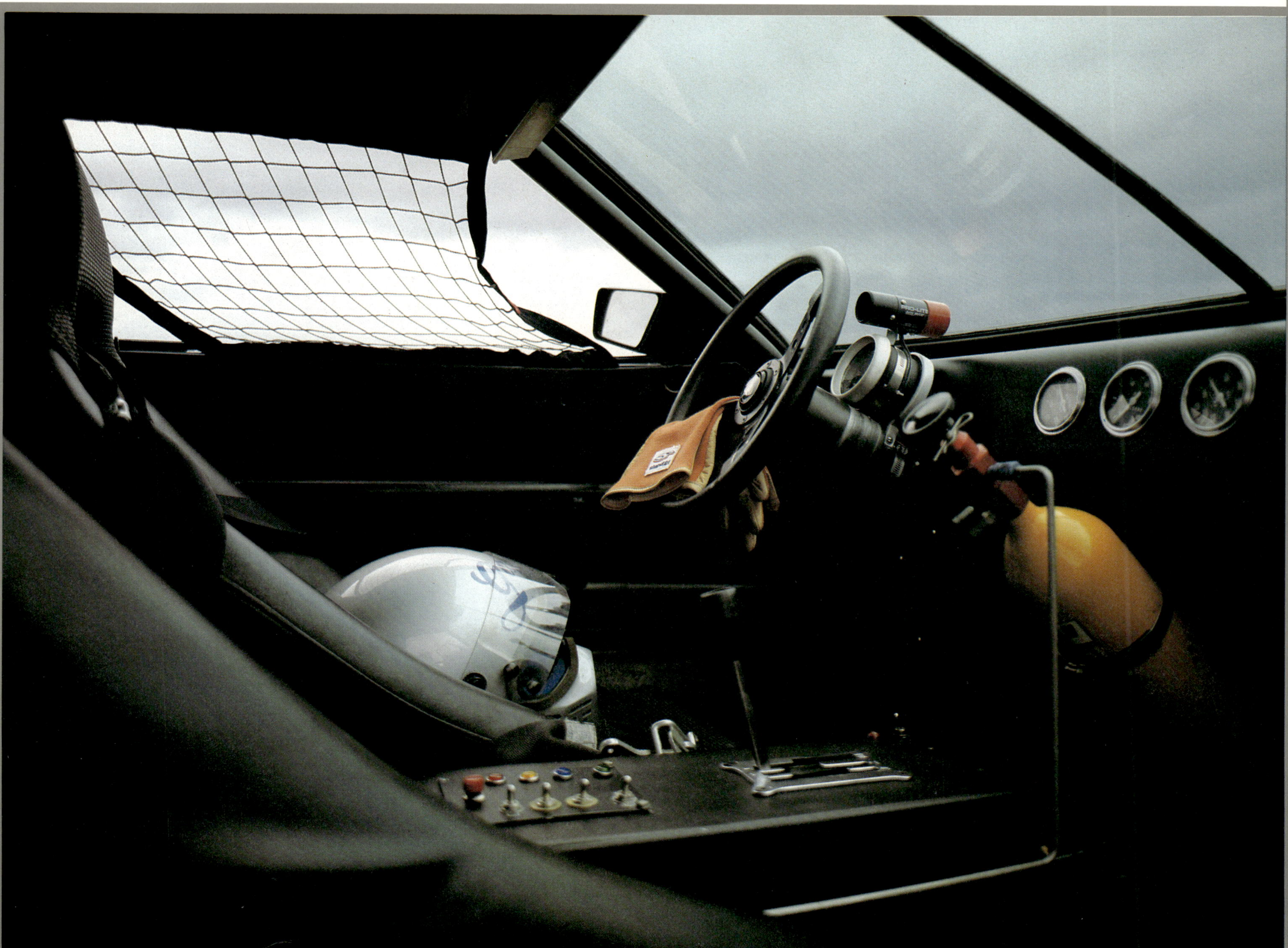

used to shake off a tailgating competitor, making him believe you're breaking earlier than you actually are.

The cockpit is enveloped in a roll cage. It's constructed by Gary, and is connected to the chassis in eleven places, adding to the rigidity. Rigidity is the name of the game when it comes to a racing chassis, he's told me. A yellow fire extinguisher is mounted on the passenger side of the console. A narrow steel tube flows from the bottle, down to the floor, out across it and back to the engine compartment. In case of fire, the driver hits the handle and powder will be jetted out over the engine and the gas tank from two strategically placed nozzles. There's a bracket in the middle of the windshield, running from the roof down to the dash, on the inside of the window. It's there to prevent the lightweight plexiglass shield from caving in at high speed. There're no side windows. Only safety nets. There to prevent the arms from being thrown out during a roll. The nets swing homely in the wind. They look like curtains. All we need now are some potted plants and it would look like *Little House on the Prairie*. Where do thoughts like that come from in moments like this?

Thumbs up! We're off! The beast grinds its teeth at first, then growls, then roars. I'm calm. Calm, like on the first bombing mission. A quick flick of the steering wheel takes us through Turn Two. Three is coming up. We're shooting through a hollow now, with grassy slopes on both sides of the track. Gary shifts to fifth, letting the clutch out quickly, purposefully, sending shivers through the chassis. We're coming up on Turn Four. Gary keeps it in fifth and under full throttle. A quick flick, a moment off the accelerator, then back on it again, smoothly, and we're through it. Gary spun here once, he told me earlier. Skidded backwards up the slope. Thought he was going to roll. He shouldn't have told me. I see why it's tricky. It's blind. But we're through! Turn Five is coming up. Just a little bend in the track. A quick flick of the wheel. Then it's uphill to Turn Six. He brakes and shifts to third. We sweep through it. The g-force feels tremendous, but the harness and the seat keep me in place. I'm calm. Gary accelerates out of the curve with the suspension bouncing and working and throws it in fourth. He lets it run up to seven thousand. He never looks at the tach, he's told me. He knows the sound of six thousand. And seven thousand. Like the back of his hand. We're shooting up a hill. I can't see the track on the other

The engine in Gary Hall's racing Pantera, pictured to the left, is a most impressive sight. Here, the velocity stacks protruding from the Webers still have their protective covers on. Above, at speed! Notice how the large front spoiler almost scrapes the track. Notice also the NACA ducts replacing the headlights. These ducts provide cooling for the front brakes. To the right, the impressive frontal view! Notice the large "ears" protruding from the empty rear side-windows. These scoops funnel air to the row of hungry Webers. The spoiler, NACA ducts and air-scoops have, after proper testing, been included in the Hall Pantera catalog. (Photographs courtesy Hall Pantera.)

side, and I've never been on it before. Which way does it turn? We fly over the crest and the combined downforce of landing and braking throws me violently into the harness. I don't care which way it goes. Gary must know! He's down to third before Turn Seven — a left-hander. He sweeps through that turn, and flicking the wheel he throws the car the other way, setting it up for Turn Seven A — this is the short track — a right-hander. He's hard on the throttle going through and out of that turn, runs it up to six thousand, shifts to fourth, runs it up to six thousand again, and shifts to fifth just as we shoot under the Champion Bridge. I lean over and see the needle closing up on seven thousand. The roar of the beast and the hissing of the wind shooting by are truly exhilarating. Something spiritual about it. I take my eyes off the track again. After all, this is the straightaway. I look at Gary. His concentration is total. He is oblivious to everything except what goes on with the car and the track. He has told me that he talks to himself, inside his head, while he drives. He's always a step ahead of the car. "Last time you apexed too late," he will say. "Make it three feet shorter this time." I look down at the speedometer in my lap. It's showing 160. We're coming up on Turn Nine, the long, sweeping, steeply banked high-speed curve before the finish-line straightaway. I see the numbered brake warning signs approaching rapidly. Four rushes by. He doesn't brake yet. I'm calm. Three. He doesn't brake. Two. He still doesn't brake! A quick glance at the speedometer in my lap tells me we're doing 175. I'm not calm anymore! He must brake! For heaven's sake! Give me a brake! Brake! Is something wrong with them? They don't work! My God! One. Now he brakes! Very hard, but for a short moment only. We're going through Turn Nine at 150, keeping about fifteen feet up from the inner edge, accelerating gradually, still running in fifth, apexing almost at the end of the turn. Just then we see the first big rain drops splashing onto the windshield. And up ahead, we see the checkered flag coming out. Gary lifts the foot off the accelerator, coasts into the pit lane and rolls lazily up along the wall until we come to a stand still. And then; Ignition off! Gloves off! Helmet off! He turns to me with a that-was-that smile.

"How did you like it?"
"It was great! Could have done it all day! Sure! But what about the brakes? What went wrong?"
"Nothing went wrong! That's how good they are! Always had to brake at Four! Now I can brake at One!"

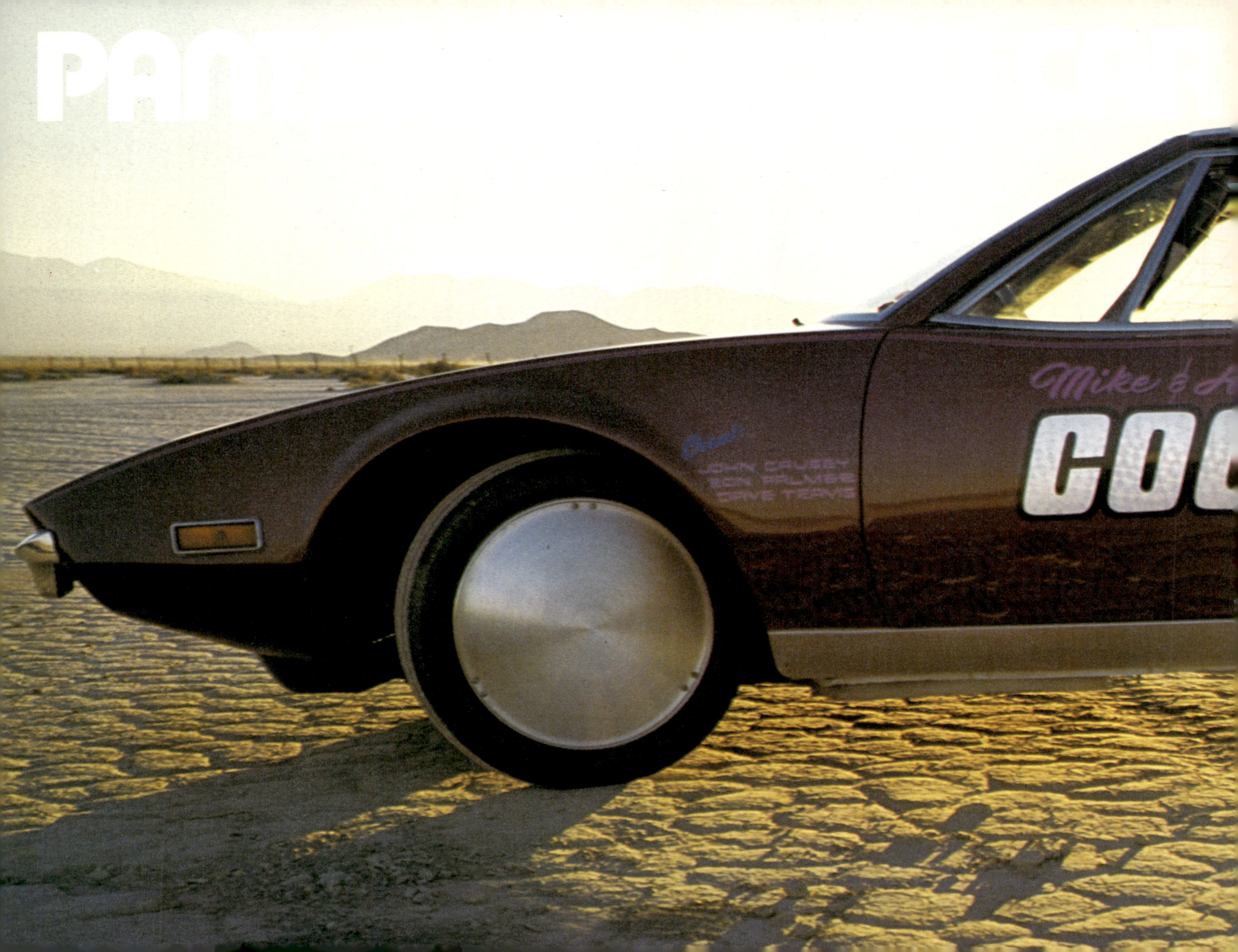
PAN
Mike &
COC

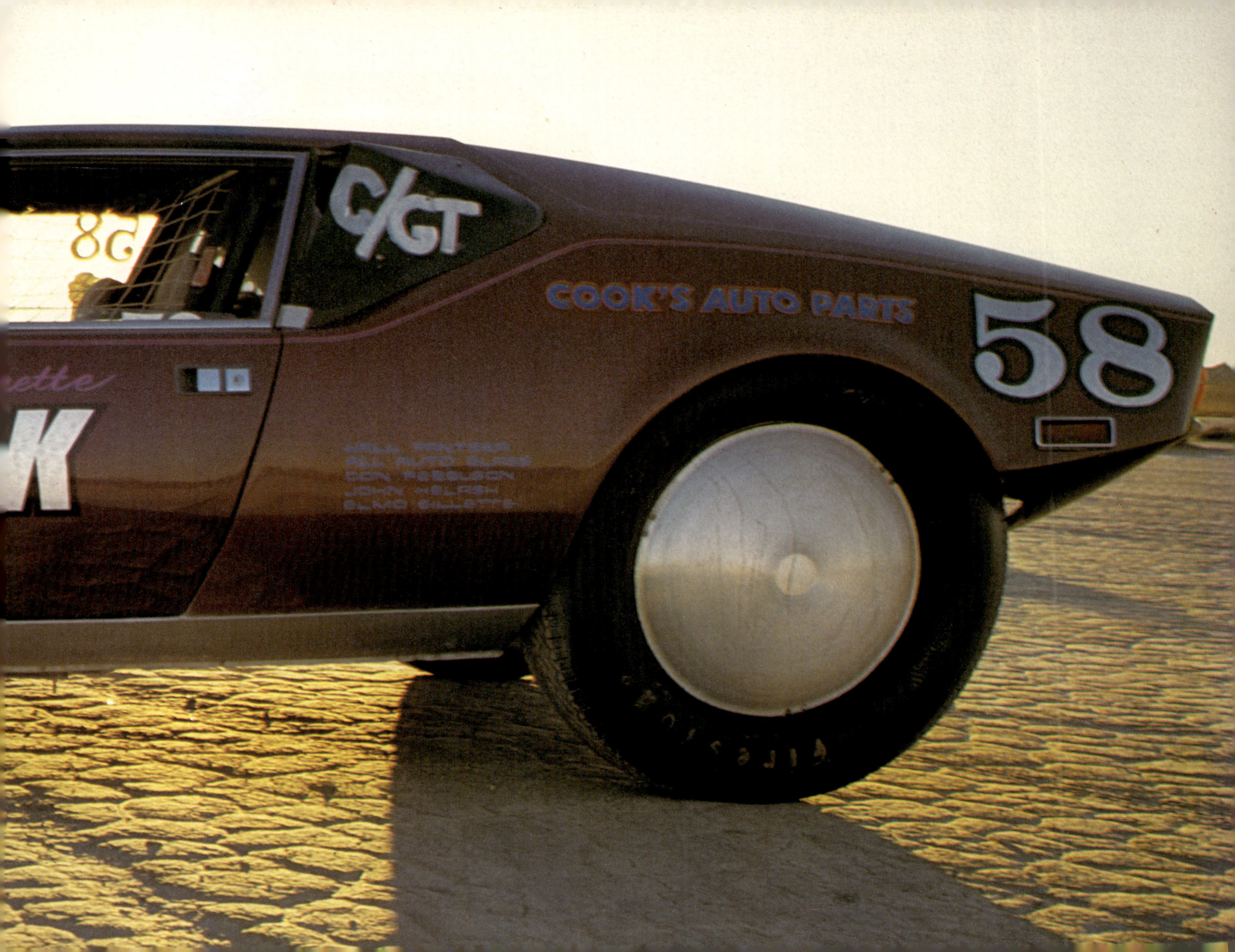
C/GT
COOK'S AUTO PARTS
58

World's Fastest Sports Car

To get there from Los Angeles, you take the San Bernardino Freeway, going south. When you hit Interstate 15, you turn inland, towards Las Vegas. There will be a gray haze obscuring the view of the mountains ahead of you. Behind you, there will be a brown, unhealthy-looking cloud of smog. But as you begin to climb, almost without noticing the incline of the road, the view will turn crisp and clear.

You will soon be climbing more dramatically — on a triple-lane freeway that conquers the mountain passes in sweeping curves of asphalt and concrete. You will keep on climbing until you reach El Cajon Summit at 4,259 feet. From there on it is clear sailing and you can coast down the hill to the valley below.

You are now in the Mojave Desert. But you have still not reached your destination. To get there, you have to take off on Highway 395, going north towards Adelanto. Just before that small, dust-ridden desert town, you turn west. The road has now become a narrow, one-lane affair.

After about ten miles you should park, turn off the engine and roll down the windows. You will be totally surrounded by the desert now — the expanse, the heat, the silence. In the spring, there will be life in the form of green foliage and flowers. In the fall, there will be death and it will come rolling across the road in the form of large dry balls of intertwined, bone-gray skeletons of lifeless vegetation.

If you had parked in this particular spot on a particular Sunday morning last fall, you would have been shaken out of your desert trance by the sudden roar of a powerful engine. As the sound increased in force, growing to a 10,000 rpm scream, you would have seen a whirling cloud of dust rise from the direction of the sound. Suddenly the sound would have died down and the cloud would have begun to settle.

Soon there would have been another roar and another cloud and you would have felt compelled to start your car and enter a narrow track to the right. Winding in and out between dead brush and dried-out river beds, it would have led you out onto the cracked

In the sport of speed record racing, it is not only important to be able to go fast, it is equally important to be able to stop fast. To the left, Mike Cook's record car has just come to a halt. After having performed its duty, the parachute rests passively on the cracked surface of El Mirage – a dry lake in the Mojave desert, east of Los Angeles. Above, the crew makes an after-the-run check. A piece of "200-mile tape" seems to have come loose, threatening to be sucked into the carburetors. Right, Mike Cook is pleased after having set a new record in his class, reaching a speed of 184 mph. (Photographs by the author.)

floor of El Mirage, a dry lake, where you would have arrived right in the middle of the speed trials sponsored six times annually by the Southern California Timing Association.

Just as you would have turned west, following a row of orange markers and slowly rolled on towards the starting line, passing the timing tower with timekeepers perched up there, Air Force caps deep on their foreheads, binoculars in straps around their necks, you would have heard another car start, and, following the direction of the sound, you would soon have discovered it on the horizon, approaching rapidly, kicking up dust, and you would have heard that scream again as the car passed the timing tower, breaking the beam of the electronic clock. Moments after that, you would have noticed a cluster of lines with a lump in the end disengage from the rear of the car. For a fraction of a second it would have been swirling and twisting in the space between the car and the dust cloud. Then you would have seen the lump unfold and blossom into a brightly colored parachute. You would have seen the car being forcably slowed down by the chute. You would have seen it roll on for another couple of hundred feet with the power shut off and the sound gone. And you would have seen it turn and slowly make its way back along the far side of the track, returning to the starting line for another run.

If the car had set a new record, you would have seen well-wishers gather around it. If things had not gone so good, only the mechanics would have been coming around in their truck. Then you would have seen them hook up the car behind the truck and pull it into one of the two lines. All the while during the stop-and-go wait, you would have seen the mechanics keep on working with the car.

On that particular Sunday, if you had been a De Tomaso enthusiast, you would have noticed with special interest a burgundy-colored Pantera in the line-up. It would have had enormously tall, but narrow, tires in the rear. In the front, the tires would also have been narrow, but of normal height. There would have been moon discs covering the wheels for improved airflow. And there would have been two large airscoops, one on each side of the rear side windows. There would also have been a large airbox protruding through the engine cover. On the outside, these alterations would have been the only things setting the car apart from a normal street Pantera.

Mike Cook, owner and driver of the Pantera, would
(continued on overleaf)

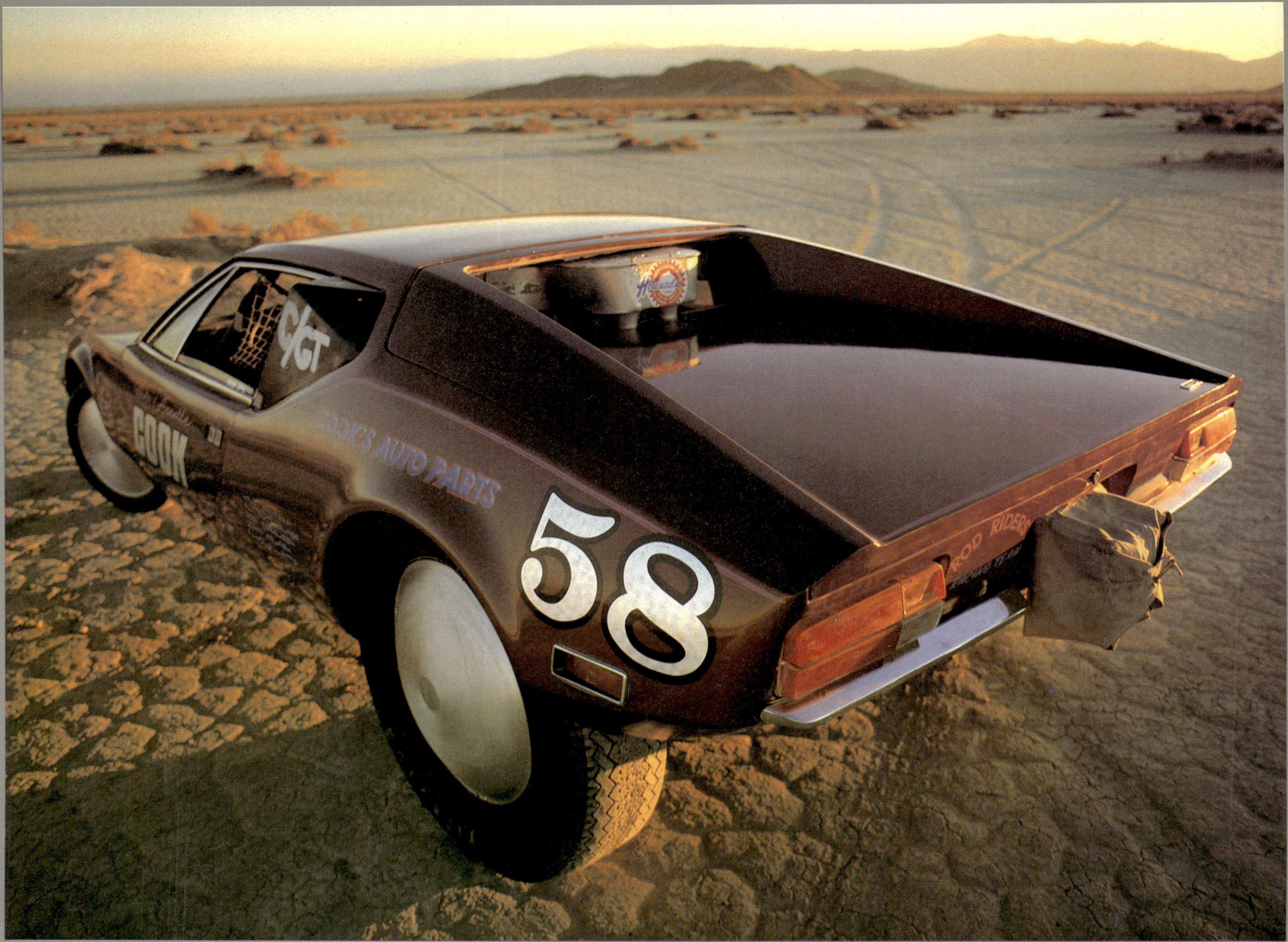
C/GT
COOK
COOK'S AUTO PARTS
58
ROD RIDERS

Racing victories were never connected with the Pantera. But, at last, now there is something for the record books: A Pantera scored the fastest time in the Grand Touring Class C at El Mirage Dry Lake, California. The new record is 184 mph! The original shape of Mike Cook's 1971 Pantera, chassis number 1581, has not been altered – proof of the outstanding inherent aerodynamics of the Pantera styling concept. The suspension, except for shorter front springs, the clutch, the transmission and the brakes, are all stock. The engine, on the other hand, has received a lot of attention. It now produces around 650 hp and can be revved up to 8500 rpm and more. Notice that a parachute is needed to stop the car!

have been behind the wheel, and on that particular Sunday, you would have seen the well-wishers gather around him. He would have just returned from setting a new record. The Pantera had been clocked doing 184 mph! The speed was recorded at the end of the 1.3-mile distance, after a standing start.

For Mike Cook of Carson, California, it all began a long time ago when he, at the age of eight, first accompanied his father to the Bonneville Saltflats. His father, known simply as "Jr.," was a successful drag racer, remaining a top contender for two decades. In 1972, father and son, who jointly operate an auto parts and service store, decided to buy a Pantera. Mike liked it so much and drove it so much that Jr. thought it was too much! Mike decided to buy his own. That was in 1975.

One Sunday, more or less out of curiosity, he entered a speed trial at El Mirage. He recorded 124 mph without having done any of the allowed alterations to the car. He now decided to try to fulfill his childhood dream of becoming a speed champion.

In his second try, still using street tires and carburetor aspiration, he ran 158 mph. He had installed Hall Pantera's Brute Power Package special camshaft, manifold and headers. He had also added a roll-bar.

Now things got progressively more serious. Regulations had him install a roll cage and a fire protection system. He also stripped off the undercoating and painted the undercarriage with slick black laquer. And he began experimenting with the airflow in the heads. He now recorded 164 mph.

For the next try, Mike constructed a fuel injection system based on Hilborn components, mounted big John Deere tractor wheels in the rear and Centerlines up front. He now also had to install a parachute. This time he captured the record with an 176-mph run.

He now continued experimenting with improved airflow in the heads, installed a larger camshaft, and beat his own record, this time recording 184 mph.

Having captured the record both in the D and C Production Classes, Mike is now going after the record in the B Production Class. One of these Sundays, if you go up to El Mirage, you will see his burgundy-colored Pantera, now with a 429 Boss engine on board, doing 220 mph! But Mike's ultimate goal is for the Pantera to become the world's fastest production car — any class! For that he has to go to Bonneville and do over 250 mph. You watch! He will do it one of these Sundays . . .

The term "a typical day at the races" is not quite correct to use in describing a speed record racing event. There are virtually no spectators, no fashionable attire, no breathtaking excitement, no champagne for the winners. Instead, there is a lot of dust, a lot of wind, a lot of dirty hands. And in place of the champagne – a handshake. Mike Cook knows how it feels to break the record. In the picture above, his Pantera is captured moments after having been clocked doing 184 mph. The parachute is effectively bringing the speed down. To the right, the Pantera is waiting for another shot at the record. To the left, as the day comes to an end, the scruteneer performs his task. (Photographs by the author.)

Panteras For The Road
The Survivors Series

"Panteras For The Road," seventh in The Survivors Series, was photographed, written and designed by Henry Rasmussen. The technical specifications in the content section were compiled and researched by Gene Babow. Assistant designer was Walt Woesner. Copy editor was Barbara Harold. Typesetting was supplied by Tintype Graphic Arts of San Luis Obispo, California. The color separations were produced by South China Printing Company of Hong Kong, which was also responsible for the printing and binding. Liaison man with the printer was Peter Lawrence of New York. A limited number of books were bound by National Bindery of Pomona.

In addition to the skilled craftsmen associated with the above mentioned firms, the author also wishes to thank the owners of the featured automobiles for their invaluable cooperation.

Special acknowledgements go to Gary Hall of Hall Pantera, Bellflower, California, for sharing so generously of his wealth of knowledge; to Bill Kosfeld of Motorbooks International, for his pleasant way of handling the day-to-day contacts connected with publishing; to Tomas Wenner of Winkel, Switzerland, for making available his knowledge of the Italian language during the author's visit to the De Tomaso factory. The author is also indebted to Tom Warth of Motorbooks International, whose continued support made this book possible.

The author finally wishes to thank the following contributors: Aurelio Bertocchi, Dick Carr, Ivano Cornia, Barry Gale, Winston Goodfellow, Beverly Hall, Robb Main, Rick McBride, Otis Meyer, Ken Morabito, Bruce Munch, Ena Rasmussen, Shirley Rusch, Bob Turney and Bill Wysock.